What's Next

An Inspiring Autobiographical Tale of Insanity and Awesomeness

Dustin J. Pari

DEDICATION

This one is for the dreamers… assuming I'm not the only one left.
And for my daughter, known affectionately as "Beans". Daddy loves you.

- Never Give Up -

CONTENTS

ACKNOWLEDGMENTS

Throughout the pages of this book you will meet many characters—some
you may even know, some who may appear as remnants of a dream you can
almost remember. To them, and to you, I am thankful.

I acknowledge God… everyone else is suspect.

FOREWORD
BY JESSICA JEWETT

When Dustin asked me to edit this literary misadventure for him, as he called it, I initially met the request with hesitation. He's a well-known paranormal investigator, yes, but he's also a well-known Christian and I wondered how his fans would receive a book edited by a vocal pagan like me. I am a practicing witch from generations of practicing witches, but as I thought about his request, I reminded myself that I'm also a professional. I have credentials as a freelance editor, an author, and a paranormal researcher in my own right, so I knew I was highly qualified to take on the job he offered.

Most importantly, however, I am Dustin's longtime friend and I know his mind, his narrative voice, and his heart better than most people do. A rush of protective instincts surged through me in the process of deciding to work with him in this professional capacity. I realized I couldn't tolerate seeing a stranger hack up Dustin's story when I was more than capable of preserving his voice throughout while polishing the language for those who chose to read it. Rejecting his job offer out of my own fear over a practicing witch editing a strong Christian man's book simply wasn't what he would have done in my shoes.

In some ways, tackling the manuscript scribbled in a Captain America composition notebook was a step in my personal what's next journey. Like the monkey clinging to a branch (you'll see that lesson soon enough), I had to be willing to let go of the safety of one branch to reach out for the next one.

I often tell Dustin that listening to his stories—he has a story for every occasion—is quite a bit like wandering through real life Candy Land. The game is a journey through color, adventure, whimsical imagery, and asks the player to use their imagination in order to win. Sometimes Dustin's thought processes meander through not only Candy Land, but detours through Chutes and Ladders as well, yet if you stick with him through the journey, you'll come out stronger in the end with lessons to help you live a better life.

It's important to understand the way Dustin's mind works as you begin reading his book. Like a wall of televisions on display at an electronics store, some screens might play a continuous loop of cartoons, while others play endless music selections spanning centuries of artists, and still others might flash literary, Biblical, or television clips at random. At first glance, Dustin's thought processes appear chaotic and scattered—and sometimes they are—but part of learning from him requires a certain amount of trust. Faith, if you will, in the way that he has faith in his God and the inherent goodness within his fellow man. Taking his hand and letting him lead you through what life has taught him will no doubt leave you a far more open and sensitive person. With the ability to feel comes compassion and with compassion comes faith.

This book is partially autobiographical and partially inspiration. Motivating people and touching lives has been Dustin's goal in the entire decade that I've called him my friend. Not everything you'll read in these pages is pretty. Your perception of familiar reality shows might shift a bit and it might make you a bit uncomfortable, but don't let go of Dustin's hand. He'll lead you to a warm place of hope after the storm in the end.

I learned things about my friend and colleague through editing this book that I hadn't expected. That's precisely how I know it's an important literary feather in his cap. Putting forth the effort to open oneself up and share the guts of positive and negative life experiences takes courage.

Beyond the courage to write it, Dustin had the courage to live it and come out a better man. Now it's up to you to examine what he has to teach and have the courage to put that first foot forward along your own journey of what's next.

Jessica Jewett
February 1, 2015

CHAPTER 1
I BELIEVE IN SMALL CHAPTERS

October 2, 2011

I write this as Delta flight DL 1112 pulls away from the gate in Atlanta, Georgia. I'm snuggled into seat 31A, left side, against the window. Normally I'm an aisle seat man, but I didn't book this flight myself and by the time I checked in online, this was the best seat available. There's an empty seat betwixt me and a nondescript college kid who is also bound for PVD. That's the airport code for Providence, Rhode Island—PVD—even though the airport is in Warwick.

The college kid in 31C is rather vanilla, but perhaps not entirely nondescript as previously noted. But this literary misadventure isn't about him. If he wants a more thorough description of himself, then he can go write his own book or simply look in the mirror and update his status on Facebook. Either way is fine with me. He's just another extra in the story of my life, as I am in his. We all have a part to play. Some of us are in the limelight, while some of us are scenery.

Don't be a tree in the play of your own life. That is rule #159.

I set all sorts of obligatory rules at obligatory times, none of which may really matter and none of which are numbered in a sequential order.

Welcome to my mind. It's a pleasant place... though rather cluttered.

So what is my book about? It's an ode to what happens when

you let go of what's safe and reach out in faith for what's next.

Before you embark upon this journey into what I'm hoping will be a lively tale of struggle, madness, inspiration, and success, you must know the essentials. You cannot fully understand and appreciate my present situation without first knowing at least a smattering of the prologue.

If Charles Dickens had penned a tale of a happy-go-lucky philanthropist who simply gave away his money and repeatedly shouted "What day is it boy?" from a window, he probably wouldn't have landed upon the bestseller's list and thus, Christmas as I know it would not be Christmas.

We have now pressurized the cabin. Prepare yourself for awesomeness.

So what is my back story? What are the essentials?

"I was born a poor black child," is how Steve Martin began his story in the epic comedy, *The Jerk*.

Me? I begin my story with a reference to the classic, *A Christmas Carol*, and the follow it up with a reference to *The Jerk*. That may actually say more about me than I think.

But why do I say these things? Maybe because that Dickens' tale and that Steve Martin movie are two of my favorite things; like whiskers on kittens, warm wooly mittens, and warm pumpkin pie with real whipped cream served to me by a petite, curvy brunette. Or maybe I mention these things because Steve Martin is on the cover of the October 2011 issue of Sky Magazine and thus staring me in the face above my in-flight tray table, which is not currently in its locked and upright position. Or maybe it is simply because an early lesson in knowing me—*truly* knowing me—is to understand that in order to navigate my fragile eggshell mind, you are going to need much more than a GPS, or a compass (if you're the world's oldest Boy Scout).

If you are a Doors fan you probably just picked up on another essential: my love of music. Music of all kinds has played such a huge role in my life. It's the tool I use to mark time and index memories. It's how I know how to feel. (If you're not a Doors fan, don't worry. I just told you that I have a love of music, which was the important part. Plus, you really should have picked up on that with my "whiskers on kittens" reference, but you were probably distracted by the pie.)

So let us call this *D. Pari Essential #1—My Spliced Memories.*

Though I wasn't born a poor black child, when someone asks me about myself, it's the first thing that comes to mind. I know it's not the literal truth but it's still my honest to goodness go-to answer. Lucky for me, my mind has advanced and evolved to produce its own neat little filter that not only keeps out dirt, but it holds back my first answer and instructs me to use the second one, always. If my brain had not done so, those people who may not have been lucky enough to take in a screening of *The Jerk* would think I was racially insensitive and not see my brilliant rehash of pure comedic genius. Lord knows I have love for all. Lord also loves a working man.

So as you can see, my memories are spliced. Everything has a pop culture reference. There's always a comparison. I'd be the worst patient to whom you'd ever administer a Rorschach test. Every memory is a little bit of my life mixed with a little bit of something I have seen, read, or heard. To be honest, most of it is one cartoon or another. I am not a proud man.

Following the map to my mind is a bit messy and slightly hypnotic, like when the boat of Oompa Loompas keep on rowing but they don't know where they're going. However, just as the good children touring the museum stood by Mr. Wonka, I ask you to stand by me. Once you get an understanding of where I'm coming from, inspiration will follow and there might even be candy... I hope.

If you've ever seen the series *Dream On* that aired on HBO in the 1990s, then you know what I mean about spliced memories. The show featured a character named Martin Tupper. I can tell you this without the aid of Google or Wikipedia even though I only saw two episodes almost 21 years ago. That, my friends, is the way my mind works. I may not be able to tell you what I did yesterday (unless there was candy or pie involved), and I may not be able to tell you what I ate for lunch, but if there is a spliced reference between an actual event and a movie title, a scene in a movie, a television show, a theme for a television show, a cartoon, a video game, or a song lyric, then— and pretty much only then—can I accurately remember. I will tell you this: figuring out ways for me to study in school was very difficult for me and often resulted in the use of perverted anagrams and/or an obscene pneumonic. Little slices of blue humor meant just for me and the studio audience in my mind, which, by the way, thinks I'm hilarious.

Back to *Dream On* and Martin Tupper. Throughout the daily

routine and comedic mishaps of this nondescript thirty-something divorcee's life, Martin often had television memories flash in his mind that directly related to his current situation. Old cowboy films, famed Hollywood love stories, sports highlights, and so on and so forth. The idea was that his parents plopped him down in front of the television as a child and instead of learning through human interaction and family experience, he learned through television.

The key difference between yours truly and Martin Tupper, besides that of him being a fictional character and the strange fact that I still relate to him twenty-something years later, is that I have a ton of great childhood memories thanks to my family and friends. But still, for some reason, if you ask me about myself, I want to tell you that, "I was born a poor black child," just for my own amusement and for those in the cheap seats in the studio audience of my mind who are somewhat complaining about the popcorn being stale. I really should get somebody on that.

Picture if you will the beginning of this sentence. I cannot even write "picture if you will" without thinking of *The Twilight Zone* because that phrase began so many episodes. *"Picture if you will"* bounces through my brain and instantly conjures up images of New Year's Eve and the great William Shatner. They usually run a marathon of the old *Twilight Zone* episodes on New Year's Eve and my favorite episode features William Shatner as a passenger on a plane who sees a creature on the wing while they are in flight.

I also had the great pleasure to meet William Shatner while we were both featured guests at DragonCon in Atlanta, Georgia, back in 2009. He was a little more "featured" than I, but I was there too, signing autographs, giving out free hugs, free advice, and wondering how the hell I'd gotten to that point in my life. I remember thinking I'd also like to someday film my own version of William Shatner's cover of Elton John's "Rocket Man". That was truly something to behold. What moxie!

See? Did you see what happened there? Mental dominoes, my friends. It's like this all day in the elite suite betwixt my ears. It's amazing I ever get anything done. Those reading this book may even be concerned with run-on sentences. I say *pshaw*! I have a run-on mind.

One thought clicks off a spliced memory of reality and fiction that then tumbles into another, into another, into another. But that is the complex beauty of my insanity.

That, my friends, is *D. Pari Essential #1*.

Understanding the inner workings of a mind decorated with clips of cartoons whilst displaying random movie plots from many moons ago; the floor of my inner being is sticky with stray lines of dialogue and spilled Icee drinks, and all of this is backed with the ever looping theme song from *The Facts of Life*.

My days are rarely dull to say the least.

CHAPTER 2
BRIGHT LIGHTS—LOUD MUSIC—FLYING PIGS

I was born a poor... wait a minute!

I was born the son of a cross-country truck driver and secretary-turned-housewife in the era of the great all-American housewives. Lord knows I'm all for equality in the workplace and in all aspects of life, but I will go to my grave believing that raising a child and a family is the single most important responsibility a person can ever undertake. Currently many families have working moms and dads, single moms and single dads, two dads, two moms, and single grandparents. You name it, we have it. They're all out there busting their humps, doing the best they can to make a living, be a provider, and a parent. But when I was born, my father was still clinging to that Donna Reed ideal he had seen on television. The husband works, the wife takes care of everything else, preferably in pearls. And take care of everything else is what my mom did, including raising me—both of us without the pearls. My hat, though I seldom wear one, is off to her and everyone else out there who has raised a child against unknown odds and varying circumstances. Getting by in the 1970s when I was a wee tot was no cake walk, and it sure as hell isn't any easier today.

My own experience as a parent has proven to be the most enjoyable thing I've ever ventured to do, but also the most difficult in terms of providing and balancing my time. I'd like to spend every moment of every day with my daughter as she grows, but the good people at the bank who hold the note on my house wouldn't allow it—the bastards.

Outside of my television career on *Ghost Hunters* and *Ghost Hunters International*, I still do a lot in the paranormal field, including a series of college lectures, private and public events, and private cases helping people with paranormal issues. Aside from the paranormal field, I run an online ministry called The Patch Ministry where I try to help people with matters of faith, and I do all of this while holding down two jobs, one full-time and one part-time for the better part of the year. I often get up at 5 am, hit the gym, work my first job as an anesthesia technician from 8 'til 4 and then I work as a camera operator for the Pawtucket Red Sox from five 'til whenever the game ends. Then I get up and do it again the next morning.

Lather—rinse—repeat.

I stole that from a bottle of hair conditioner that borrowed it from a shampoo bottle he knew pretty well. It seems to echo my life. Plus, I love washing my hair. I prefer coconut shampoo as it makes me feel like my hair is on vacation on some fictitious tropical isle where the ladies still wear coconuts on their heaving, tanned bosoms while making pies. (I may have watched a lot of *Gilligan's Island* as a child. I still love you, Mary Ann!)

Where was I? Oh yes. Working, hustling, and getting by. It truly is the only way I know. I started working when I was 14 and I haven't taken many days off since. Steve Martin may have been *Born Standing Up*—a reference to his own book—but I was born hustling. I must turn over this copy of Sky Magazine as Steve Martin is hypnotizing me.

Twenty-seven hours of labor is what it took to bring me into this world, the original moment of letting go and reaching out for what's next. At the time, apparently I wasn't such a proponent of what's next and was more than happy to stay where I was, butt-naked, tucked warmly inside of a uterus, floating in a sweet satchel of amniotic fluid seasoned with just a hint of my own urine. Ah … the wonder of it all.

Anyhow, one thunderstorm and twenty-seven hours later, they finally pried me from my internal beanbag chair and held me out for the world to see in all my naked baby glory. I had a fat face, squinty untrusting eyes, and my ears were crumpled into balls on the sides of my head. I looked like an angry Japanese man that you might see at a flea market begrudgingly selling lampshades and bungee cords on a Sunday morning. But there I was, seven and some odd pounds of cranky awesomeness. Let the games begin! (Speaking of games beginning—I once filmed the Olympic Torch as it passed through Providence, Rhode Island, whilst I was a cameraman for WPRI CBS 12 and WNAC FOX 64 television.)

My earliest memories center around music, and many moments throughout my life have musical notations scribbled in the margins of my memory. I can tell you beyond a shadow of a doubt the first time I heard Bobby McFerrin's infectious "Don't Worry, Be Happy". I had just stepped into my mother's silverish-blue Toyota Camry as she picked me up from Monsignor Bove Elementary School on Branch Avenue in Providence in the fall of 1988. But what did I eat for breakfast yesterday? Your guess is as good as mine. Ostrich legs with jam, possibly.

I remember dancing in my car seat to Barry Manilow's "Copa Cabana" in the back of my mother's brown Chevy Nova. I swear she tied a plain bagel to a string and had it tacked to the roof of the car above my car seat but she insists it was merely tethered to the crossbar of my car seat so I wouldn't drop it. I personally like my version more since it inspires the image that I was a trained seal in a traveling circus act performing a trick for a fish—or in my case, a plain bagel. I still love plain bagels, but I don't have to tie them to anything as I'm a big boy now. I still dance my ass off to Barry Manilow's vocal offerings. On the rare occasion that I'm eating a plain bagel and "Copa Cabana" comes on the radio, life is pretty much as good as it gets.

I can tell you quite matter-of-factly that I was singing along with the radio to John Lennon's "Nobody Told Me There'd Be Days Like These" as we turned off Plainfield Street in Johnston, Rhode Island, past the old Auto Exchange car lot on our way to go bowling with my uncle and my cousins in what might possibly have been my first collective memories of bowling, my uncle, and my cousins. We were still in the brown Chevrolet at the time and I had to have been just over six years of age. At the time, I thought the lyrics were, "Nobody told me I had to wear black beads," and thus sung along accordingly. At the age of four, many years later, my own daughter sang her version, "Nobody told me I had to eat these leggies." Obviously it's a tough lyric for we Paris to get a handle on at a young age, but it may in fact be our only true weakness.

As an elementary school student sporting a Catholic school

uniform consisting of two shades of blue and an optional tie, which I did voluntarily wear early on as I always looked for a way to separate myself from the pack, to stand out and to be extra fancy, I did pretty well in my fashionable efforts and my studies. Peering out from beneath my bowl cut at a classroom all day was terribly boring for me and so I sat at my desk in the back of the room singing quietly to myself. My internal radio is almost always switched on and commercial free for the most part. However, my singing was apparently not quiet enough since numerous parent-teacher conferences were scheduled throughout my elementary career in a brave effort to squelch my vocals and ongoing distraction to the other students.

High school came and went. I embraced The Beatles, 1980s glam rock bands, Pink Floyd, and Metallica as my shepherds for grades nine through twelve. I could only half-heartedly embrace grunge rock and alternative music because I held it responsible for killing all the hard partying, eager-to-please ladies of the 80s that I thought I'd get to experience in high school. Instead, those girls were replaced by spoiled rich kids wearing baggy thrift shop clothing, smelling like patchouli, with a maddening apathy toward everything they didn't already hate. What a total letdown.

I played the bass guitar for our school rock band and I was even able to dabble in some backing vocals for a cover of "Rocking the Casbah". In my mind, it's still a legendary performance and whispered about as a myth of pure awesomeness in the hallowed halls of LaSalle Academy. In truth, it was probably very forgettable.

I did attend my first concert whilst in high school—Pink Floyd at Foxboro Stadium in Massachusetts. It was everything I wanted my first concert to be- from bright lights, loud music, to a flying pig. There was even a strangely whimsical fellow of Native American descent who stood in the row in front of my friends and me. He had a bag of brownies, danced a lot before the concert started, and then magically disappeared. We also had an unwanted interaction with a gentleman in a clearly altered state of mind who had an odd affection for the word "poster". I still don't quite understand it.

Fast forward many years later and I am dubbed "The Paranormal Rockstar" after an international phone interview for a paranormal magazine. The whole thing originated as we conversed about my personal struggle to be a good provider for my family, yet having to be so far away in order to do so. Due to my extensive world travel (and incredible taste for 80s rock fashion) I was told that I might someday tell my daughter that I lived life on the road and traveled the world as a "Paranormal Rockstar".

Well, I do love ripped up jeans and cheap screen printed t-shirts, and with my years of experience in marketing and advertising, I know a good idea when I hear one, hence "The Paranormal Rockstar" was born, branded and I became the leader of Rockstar Nation, which was the title given to my friends, supporters, and followers throughout various social media sites.

The bottom line is music played an immense part in who I am, how I look at life, how I live my life, and how I express myself. It's what moves me to move others. It's what plays in the background of my daily madness. It's where I hear God speaking to me and guiding me. Music is what got me through boring classes and helped me to catch that damn bagel on a string no matter what it was tied to.

And because of music, imagery, and fashion imitation, the Paranormal Rockstar image was born, many years after the 27 hours of labor brought me onto this stage. The Rockstar image brought about an idea, an inspirational concept to help others, to walk in faith, to let go of fear, and to reach out boldly into the limelight for what's next. Whether people like you or not, you'd better at least make sure they know you're on stage.

CHAPTER 3
WHAT ONCE WAS

October 7, 2011

Southwest flight 3780 is taxying for takeoff. I'm headed to Texas.

Time for some history. Long before I was a good Christian soldier, I indulged in the more material aspects of this life. I still love classic American muscle cars and a well-crafted adult beverage on a hot summer's day or a crisp fall evening. But I no longer party in excess—rather focusing on a more spiritual, family oriented lifestyle with an emphasis on love, truth, and inspiration. However, it was all born out of the ashes. When I felt the most broken was when things finally took shape.

After college, I held many jobs—a theme that would run throughout my life. Most of the time, it was out of pure financial necessity, while other times it was out of habit; either way, I don't sit idle long. As they say: "Idle hands spend time at the genitals, and you know how much God hates that."

I studied television and radio production whilst enrolled at the New England Institute of Technology in Warwick, Rhode Island. I enjoyed my courses and started interning at a local television station and an FM radio station, while working as a board operator at an AM radio station, producing traffic reports for the morning commute, delivering pizzas at night, and shelving books for Barnes & Noble on weekend mornings. I was running myself ragged and sadly found the best sleep I was getting was at red lights. It was time for a change.

They say luck is what happens when hard work meets opportunity. I just say thank you and try not to ask too many questions. And so it was, on New Year's Eve of 1997 when the show editor for the local CBS/Fox newscast didn't show up. I was called in and subsequently hired as a video editor for the nightly news at Fox 64/CBS 12 in Rhode Island.

Through the years, I worked my way up the ranks, going from editing one show a day to two shows, to editing a show and shooting a story, to being a full-time photographer/news videographer/what have you. I then learned to operate the live vehicle, both microwave and satellite trucks. All was well, I bought a home, but I grew bored. To already have reached a substantial goal and only be in my early twenties left me wanting more.

Operating the live vehicles left me with ample downtime, which I used to read and work on my writing. Throughout college, my professors told me that I put pen to paper like Norman Mailer. Personally, I never saw the comparison since I mostly read Chuck Palahniuk and the works of America's favorite Jewish cowboy in Texas, Kinky Friedman. Poetry, short stories, and social commentary satire were what I fancied most and thus spent countless hours in the back of a van on a cold winter's night scribbling furiously in my notebooks.

I enjoyed a steady paycheck and a more than ample social life, but I still felt empty inside. There I was—young, healthy, and doing a job that many would like to have, yet I still somehow felt dejected. Going to work became a burden and no amount of Miller High Life could deaden the sound of the news pager that beckoned me to the station on my days off.

September 11, 2001, was a day that changed the world for many reasons. The lives lost that fateful day in the skies of New York City and the ground below were a tragic turning point in American society, the ripples of which would be felt the world over.

I laid in my bed that morning, trying to rest up from work the night before. My cell phone rang and the news pager vibrated. All too often when things happen at the same time like that, they are of the negative variety. I received the horrifying news of the devastation and turned on the television as the second plane hit the side of the tower. I got dressed and went to work, glued to the radio and searching the skies.

In the days that followed, I became more and more amazed at the selflessness of the firefighters and the EMT workers. Suddenly I had a goal—a new ambition—and a fire inside me to grow, to evolve, and to achieve what's next.

Soon I enrolled in a course beginning my training in Emergency Medicine Services. I found my studies fascinating and the idea of being able to do something helpful and heroic even more so.

To this day, my personal emails all conclude with the quote, "I am looking for a 'dare to be great' situation," which was spoken by John Cusack in the film, *Say Anything….* And it's true, very true for me. I like—make that *love*—to do things for others. Things they couldn't do for themselves and things for which they could never repay you. Selfless acts. Acts of kindness, beauty, and love. And so in every moment of every day I wait and I watch for that perfect moment to step in and step up when no one else wants to or can.

Our society has become so very focused on the self. I refer to it in my ministry lectures as the iMentality, playing off of the "i" products and marketing that Apple made famous. Connecting us to each other more than any other society in history has, in turn, caused us to isolate ourselves in a self-absorbed, self-centered, compartmentalized world where all we clamor for anymore is fifteen gigabytes of fame.

But I should step down from my soapbox and return to our story. We were talking about achieving what's next, which at that time was driving me away from news and putting a chapter of my life in the rear view mirror.

Becoming an Emergency Medical Technician went well. I passed my exam at the Community College of Rhode Island and I was certified as a nationally registered EMT-B (Basic). At the basic level, for those unfamiliar with it, we're certified in basic life support including airway management, bleeding control techniques, assistance in emergency childbirth situations, and techniques to safely lift and move patients.

Finding work wasn't as easy as passing the test. My schedule at the news station fluctuated wildly and thus finding an ambulance company to work for didn't prove easy. How could I leave a solid gig I had known for many years and just jump into something brand new that I might not have been any good at? I still had a mortgage to pay and numerous other financial obligations. What if I had quit the station and found out I was a horrible EMT despite the best intentions? I was great as a news photographer; quick, reliable, artistic, and easy to work with, yet I was dying on the inside, emotionally and psychologically drained more and more every day by what I was forced to endure. Day after day of murder stories, corrupt politicians, and blatant ratings-driven nonsense had me on the ropes.

I have recognized that when I need a sign, a prophet of my own prophecy, a thumbs up from the big guy upstairs—He does provide for me but always in the strangest of ways and means sure to get my attention.

I was watching one of those daytime talk shows—not by choice, as I was a hostage audience in the waiting room of my physician. Just the annual checkup and oil change—nothing to raise an eyebrow over. The television droned on and on. I tried not to listen. An old lady next to me coughed up a huge ball of phlegm into her dainty rose Kleenex. I tried to keep in mind that she was somebody's daughter, prom date, broken heart, wife, and mother. It's sad that all the glorious things we do in life do nothing to shepherd our physical lives to a more pleasant end, but at least the soul shines on. I tried to thumb through *Sports Illustrated* but it was last year's football preview, and in hindsight, they didn't even pick the Super Bowl matchup. The old lady coughed again. More slime in the tissue.

I looked up to the television as the director in a far off studio cut to camera three and the guest, an actor from the daytime soap opera, *Passions*, now deceased—both the actor and the soap opera—turned and spoke directly through the camera, through the lens, and into my soul as he said, "If you're not happy doing what you're doing—don't do it."

There it was. Clear as day. If you're not happy doing what you're doing, simply don't *do* it. "Right on the target—so direct," as Bob Dylan penned in the soulful song, "You're Gonna Make Me Lonesome When You Go".

Speaking of Mr. Zimmerman, aka Dylan, his album *Blood On The Tracks* has to be one of the most influential albums in the soundtrack of my life. That also happened by accident. After my senior year of high school, my family purchased a home that was undergoing renovations, so I opted to spend that summer living with my Uncle Frank—known affectionately as Uncle Bub—for what would be a pivotal point in my emotional maturation and understanding of this world. Uncle Bub is legendary amongst my friends. He specialized in living his life in shades of gray; that is to conform enough to acquiesce to mainstream standards, yet rebel enough to keep a shine on his soul and a song in his heart.

Many of those songs were that of Bob Dylan played on the aging kitchen radio's cassette deck. Many a morning featured me complaining about his musical selection, calling Dylan unintelligible but as the summer progressed, I began sitting with him many a late night singing along to Bob Dylan whilst Uncle Bub strummed his acoustic guitar. One of those songs found on the *Blood On The Tracks* album is "Simple Twist Of Fate" and it is in that sentiment that our tale continues.

It was a simple twist of fate that caused me to be late getting to the newsroom in East Providence that day; be it from a traffic light, an errant motorist cutting me off, or simple a last-minute trip to clear my bladder before leaving for work. Something caused me to set into the newsroom a few minutes late and thus the reporter and story got assigned to a different photographer, which resulted in me being assigned to "cruise for news". This assignment meant I loaded up the SUV with my gear, turned on the police scanners, and drove around the state waiting for the next big thing. Truth be told, I usually cruised with the radio turned up and the scanners turned off. Sometimes I even stopped by my favorite watering hole for a quick 16 or 24 ounces of liquid sunshine. Come to think of it, perchance I went to work late on purpose as cruising for news was obviously the better gig—at least if you did it my way.

On that particular night, I was driving up to Colt State Park in Bristol; a beautiful spot by the ocean filled with verdant pastures embracing hope, daydreams, and moments of magical whimsy experienced all too few in this life. I had spent countless days and nights as a child in that park. I flew kites with my mother. I went fishing by lantern light with my father. In high school, I would park my 1990 Dodge Daytona ES around the first bend, walk over to a single tree that stood alone in a field, beneath which I'd write poetry, ponder life, and nap. Many great memories are still being created in that park as I pen this literary misadventure. I take my daughter there to fly kites, to run, to explore, and to dream. I don't take her to fish as it just seems cruel to trick a fish onto a hook only to rip it out again and return the bewildered creature back into the sea.

Back to the lecture at hand. I was cruising up to the park when my cellphone rang. It was the news desk asking me to head up that way as the police were just called to a murder scene.

As fate would have it, I was literally one street away from the scene. I arrived before the police and sat in my vehicle waiting— thinking as an EMT while I watched the ambulance arrive. Out of respect to the victim and their family, I'll willingly leave out the details. Just know it was heart wrenching.

The cops taped off the scene. The coroner covered the body and placed it on a stretcher. As they closed the ambulance doors, I reached down and turned on my camera for the first time. The other stations had filmed the whole time and so it was no surprise to me when the vibration of my news pager awoke me the next day from a dream I don't recall but I'm certain was better than my reality.

As we continue this story, understand that, like monkeys, many of us only release one branch once we have a firm grip on the next one. This unwillingness to release what's in our grasp, what's now, what's safe, is what this book is all about. If we cannot live in faith, we cannot let go and reach out for what's next. A loving God will get you where you need to go, regardless of where you are and what you think. This is not to say we should act irrationally and conduct ourselves as fools, but it is to say you cannot reach for what you want if you're too afraid to lose what you have. And faith is that invisible, intangible thing that will get you from what's now to what's next in your life.

At the time I was an unwilling little monkey, and for me, letting go of what was safe and easy, even though I knew I wasn't happy and I had just been told, "If you're not happy doing what you're doing— don't *do* it," seemed impossible. And so, this little monkey had to be pushed off the branch.

"Call in to the station immediately," the pager said. As I read it, my cell phone rang. I knew enough that these two things happening at once meant bad news, so I didn't answer the phone nor did I follow the command given to me via text message. I stand firm in answering to only one boss, and He talks to me in my heart. The rest of my "bosses" are obeyed only out of respect if they deserve it. The title "boss" without respect is merely a title. I can call myself the Mayor of Popsicle Town if I want to, but if the good citizens of

Popsicle Town don't respect me and garner me the authority one should have as Mayor of Popsicle Town, then it's an empty title even if I wore a monocle, top hat, and a proper beauty pageant style mayoral sash.

The leader of the newsroom shall have his name forgotten in this book, as it will be from numerous future books, I would imagine, if he has not changed his ways. It's not for me to judge. Judging is nasty stuff that I'd rather not sully my fingers with so I will leave that to God. For the purpose of wrapping up this chapter of what once was, let's call him Mr. Downtown.

When I ankled it into the newsroom at my scheduled time, Mr. Downtown emerged from his office like the first turd out of your bottom after a very long ride home. I was ordered into his fish tank of an office. I waved polite hellos to my friends as I followed Mr. Downtown to his desk. Let's say he politely asked if I was first on the scene. He didn't do it politely but since I'm a nice guy, let's say he did. I told him I was and left it at that.

"Where is the video of the body? Where is the video of the sheet draped gurney? Where? Where?" Those were the majority of his questions. I admitted that I didn't shoot that as I felt it inappropriate, regardless of what the other stations had. I was politely told that I had no "killer instinct" to which I replied my feelings that Mr. Downtown had no moral compass. He didn't like that.

What followed was a profanity laden tirade that may still hang over the newsroom to this day. I sat quietly since I didn't like profanity and I still apologize for my use of it on occasion. His speech concluded with calling me a troublemaker who wore "rock 'n roll t-shirts" and to this day my friends and I still joke about what insinuation lived behind "rock 'n roll t-shirts". As for the troublemaker, I choose to think of myself as more of a liberator, or Mayor of Popsicle Town and sometimes the Wizard of Awesome.

He may have had a point with that one. I did cause him trouble by liberating others. Here's a quick example. I used the interoffice memo system on the computer to inspire others with memos entitled, "Hey Yo..." These writings were often simple observations about life meant to brighten people's days as we all muddle through somehow. One particular day, I wrote, "Tomorrow is going to be 80°. Life is short. How many sick days do you have left?" This resulted in a very large amount of people taking the following day off, and because of this sheer coincidence, I was deemed a troublemaker or liberator depending on your perspective.

Okay, there was this one other incident where I repeatedly left the rules to *Fight Club* on the office copy machine. I'm guilty of awesomeness. I admit it.

Back to the fish tank office. Mr. Downtown asked what he was supposed to do with me. I've always despised this practice. I told him he didn't have to do anything because I was leaving in two weeks. He was stunned. I took his silence to mean our little meeting was adjourned and thus took my leave of the fish tank office.

For some very lucky viewers of the Rhode Island and Bristol County viewing area, this next part must have been a rare treat, however strange it may have appeared.

I'm sure as you have seen on various news programs, many stations have at one time or another cut into their own newscast with the tease of an upcoming story by a reporter located back in the newsroom. Why they wouldn't just let the anchor read the tease or invite the troll reporter in from the newsroom, I just don't know. I understand it's supposed to be more gritty and real and great for ratings, but it always seemed silly and not exciting. On this particular day, it did prove exciting in many ways.

As I exited the fish tank, the director in the control room down the hall unknowingly cut to camera four as I walked behind the reporter in the newsroom. As he read his tease, the people at home witnessed me saunter through the background followed by a suddenly animated and irate Mr. Downtown shaking his sweaty dumpling of a fist and bellowing a single phrase that continually propels me to do more and achieve what's next.

"You'll never win, Pari!"

God bless you, Mr. Downtown. I hope you found your moral compass and with it happiness.

CHAPTER 4
WHAT ONCE COULD HAVE BEEN

October 10, 2011

The stewardess on Southwest flight 2141 is closing the overhead cabin doors. Our Boeing 737 aircraft is preparing to take me from Austin, Texas, to Chicago, Illinois, on my way home from yet another paranormal conference. Once again, I spoke about what's next in regards to my future and urged people to find the what's next their lives. I'm never sure if I'm successful. I just plant the seed and hope it grows. Now we return to our story and read what once could have been.

After leaving the news station, I started working at a full-time gig as an Emergency Medical Technician for a private ambulance company. The bulk of the transports were for patients being admitted to hospitals from nursing homes or patients being admitted to nursing homes from hospitals. There was also a steady rotation of patients that required transport to and from dialysis treatments each week.

Most of the guys I worked with were already firefighters and just took a few EMT shifts to pick up extra hours and make a little cash. The rest of us were working towards being firefighters, making some money, and taking our classes to become cardiac level EMTs, or EMT-C, which was required in order to become a firefighter in Rhode Island. The difference between an EMT-B and EMT-C was the ability to read cardiac rhythms, start IVs, push various medications, and use the defibrillator—or shock paddles.

As I worked toward my cardiac certification, I picked up as many shifts as possible at the ambulance company and started to volunteer at a local fire station. Being the new guy at the station, I didn't do or say much. I cleaned a lot of things, worked out a lot, and slept. As my hours increased at the ambulance company, I was at the station less and less, and eventually not at all. There was plenty of overtime work available, so I was busy and my wallet was fat. Life was good.

Things at the ambulance company were going well. Unlike a lot of people I worked with who seemed jaded and at times down right uncaring for the patients, I enjoyed talking with them and trying to comfort them while they rode with me.

Many patients were noted as "frequent fliers" because we saw them regularly going in and out of the hospitals and nursing homes. I made an effort to get to know a little bit about each of them, often asking questions about loved ones and trying to match names with faces upon their walls or in frames by their bedsides. There were a few people whom I worked with who seemed to have this same mindset, viewing our elderly patients as someone's grandmother or grandfather and treating them with respect. Others unfortunately treated them as burdens and might as well have been delivering pizzas rather than tending to someone in need with help and comfort.

At the other end of the spectrum lurked some dangerous characters that wanted to play doctor while on a transport, always wanting to start IVs, give fluids, and push medications. Those people frightened me the most. Being in Rhode Island, especially serving the Warwick area, every nursing home was within a quick fifteen to twenty minute ride from a hospital, so the need to do such workups on fragile patients was minimal. The majority of the patients were being admitted for testing or for suffering a fall from bed. Few needed immediate treatment from a part-time wannabe hero bouncing along in the back of an ambulance.

I can say that in my years of working as an EMT, I started an IV twice on a patient and used the lights and sirens less than a dozen times, as most of my calls just required safe transport, careful watch, and a sympathetic ear. I did my job well and was promoted to operations manager, dealing with schedules and licensing requests, supplies, and vehicle maintenance. Being in the office was all right. The pay was good, the work was easy, and I still did some patient runs to keep from getting bored. Months passed and I continued taking various written exams for the departments hiring new firefighters, and just waiting for the call.

Staying in shape is of the utmost importance. Down in Quonset by the old Naval base, they held the physical certification testing. It is quite difficult if you're not in good condition. You have to wear a weighted vest, pick up a bundle of hose, and run it up two flights of stairs. Then you have to put it down, pick up another bundle, and carry it back down the stairs. You then drag a length of hose a distance across the floor. You have to simulate ax chopping by using a sledgehammer and driving a weighted block a measured distance beneath your feet while standing on a raised platform. Then you hoist a bundle of hose two stories up into the air by using a rope and pulley system. Then you finish by dragging a 150 pound dummy a measured distance designated by the administrator. Did I mention all of this has to be done within a certain time limit? And everyone there knows if you don't finish under five minutes, you probably will not be high on a fire company's list to call.

The night before the test, instead of going to bed early and getting some rest, I went out with my friends to have a few beers. At the time, I would have said I did it because I was nervous. I can honestly tell you I did it out of fear. I couldn't face the possibility that I might not be able to finish the test—never mind finishing it in under five minutes. I figured I could blame it on going out the night before if I didn't pass the test.

The morning came just the same and I drove my '99 Mazda pickup to Quonset. I remember the uneasy feeling in my stomach when they snapped on the vest. The weight on my shoulders was nothing compared to that in my heart.

"You'll never win, Pari," echoed throughout the cluttered corridors of my mind.

I stood nervously with the first bundle of hose at my feet. Maybe I should have filmed the dead body. Maybe I had no killer instinct. Maybe I wouldn't ever win.

The administrator clicked his stopwatch and I was off in a flash. Carrying and dragging the hose were no big deal as I had practiced these tasks many times before. The overhead ax chop was difficult for me though. No matter how many times I've tried before, I could never quickly dispatch the weighted block between my feet as fast as I wanted it.

Bang, bang, went the hammer.

I could feel my blood pounding through my veins. I could hear the stopwatch ticking in my mind. I thought of being in the fish tank office at the newsroom.

Bang, bang.

Mr. Downtown's words were trying to strangle me.

Bang, bang. ·

I was making more progress now. I used my anger. I used the hate in his words to motivate me further.

I finished the ax chop and dispatched the rest of the course without much difficulty. I did it. And, I did it in under five minutes. I went outside and I put both hands on the chain-link fence next to my truck and I threw up onto the green grass below.

In my head, Mary Tyler Moore threw her hat into the air.

"You're going to make it after all!"

With my cardiac license, my under five minute time, and a high-grade on the written exam, I applied to every department I could and made the list for one down in the town of Smithfield. All I had to do now was wait.

In the meantime, I took a position at a facial and oral surgeon's office. They hired EMT-Cs, and with some training and supervision, used them to assist in surgery administering various medications for sedation and monitoring the vital signs of patients throughout the procedures. It was interesting work in an interactive environment and since sedations were only done in the mornings, it allowed me to continue working full-time at the ambulance company until the call came from the Smithfield Fire Department. I achieved my goal—or so I thought.

I awoke one morning to find I was numb from my hips to my knees. I could walk fine, but my back was in excruciating pain and my legs were tingling. Not good.

A trip to my physician, several co-pays, x-rays, and scans later, I was told I had two discs in my lower lumbar region of my back that were severely swollen—plus the pain and the pressure of said discs upon the nerves was causing the numbness.

You remember when the doctor told Mrs. Gump that her son,

Forrest, had a spine shaped like a question mark? Well, when I was a child, a doctor told Mrs. Pari that her son had a back that curved quite dramatically too. I was born with scoliosis and up until that fated day, it had never been too much of an issue. But there I was, in pain, yet numb, and worried.

My doctor recommended physical therapy and the usual assortment of designer narcotics pushed by the pretty little drug representative who took him to lunch and made him feel like the prettiest girl at the clinic. I filled my prescription. I made my appointment. I went home.

Then I was notified by the Smithfield Fire Department that very day that my number had come up on the list and to come in for my psychological evaluation so we could get the process started. This was the call I was waiting for—and now there was nothing I could do about it. Sure, I could have simply said nothing and hoped somehow they wouldn't find out about my back. Rehabilitating my injury and therapy sessions may be able to help me fake it for a little while. Not wanting to give up, I made the psychological exam appointment and hoped my back would mend.

By the time the psychological exam came, I was feeling better. The numbness in my legs had long since disappeared and the pain in my lumbar was minimal if anything at all. Maybe Mary Tyler Moore was right. I was going to make it after all.

I was to report to the fire station after working at the surgeon's office that morning. I had taken the time off from the ambulance company and it wasn't a big deal because I worked in the office anyway and made my own schedule. I was saying goodbyes at the end of my morning shift as I normally did. One of the women I worked with was in the back room putting away a stock shipment that just came in. She asked me if I could put the case of gloves up on the top shelf for her because she couldn't reach that high. As I bent down to pick up the box—a box that couldn't weigh more than 12 or 15 pounds—my back went out. I couldn't even straighten up fully. The pain was excruciating.

So I had to call and cancel my psychological evaluation. They removed me from the hiring list.

In my heart, I didn't want to do it. I was so close to what I had worked years for and yet, "You'll never win, Pari," was driven through my heart like a blade. But as much as I wanted it, I knew I couldn't live with myself if I was on a call for the fire department and my back went out. What if that box of gloves was a child in a building burning to the ground? What would happen then?

Sometimes we think we know our destiny. We think our dreams belong to us when in fact we are a small part of a much bigger picture that we're not painting and not privy to even glimpse.

I was deeply saddened for some time, though most around me probably never knew it. "We keep on keeping on," sang Ziggy Marley, son of the great Bob Marley.

It needs to be noted that I didn't give up on my goals. I did everything I could in effort to make it happen. Chiropractors, therapy, core strengthening workouts—nothing could change the fact that I was born with a curved spine that sometimes kept me upright and other times rendered me immobile.

Thankfully, as of this writing, the latter of the two is rare indeed. Over the years, I have strengthened myself to where 99% of the time, my back isn't an issue at all but there are still those days that it acts up and reminds me of that first morning when my legs were numb. When I'm a weathered old memory of the man I am today, riding in the back of an ambulance, getting prodded needlessly with needles, my back probably will not be so great, but we must accept the things we cannot change.

It is time to restore my tray table to its upright and locked position. After a quick layover in Chicago, a trip to the urinal, and the food court, we will return to our regularly scheduled program.

CHAPTER 5
TWISTS AND TURNS OF FATE

Southwest flight 237 is thundering up the runway and taking me back home.

When we last left our hero, he had to accept what was simply not to be, and he was unsure of what he was to become. And now, we return to our story.

I continued working two jobs because that's what I know how to do and I took some comfort in doing so. "Just gettin' by on gettin' by's my stock in trade," sang Jerry Jeff Walker.

I worked surgery by day, ambulance by night, and often overnight since those shifts paid well. As Rick Ross sang, "Every day, I'm hustling." There were at least two or three days a week when I could only go home to shower and then return to one office or another, all the time unsure of where I was headed or why.

Despite my 60-plus-hour work week, I still maintained a very comfortable social life and was far from lonely, yet somehow always empty.

As cliché as it may sound, one morning I awoke to the sound of church bells and felt an inner urgency which I still cannot describe fully or accurately. I needed to return to church and rediscover my faith, possibly for the first time.

I was raised a good little Christian boy at Monsignor Bove School on Branch Avenue in Providence, a school known for churning out good little Christian boys and girls. That was followed up by four years of study at LaSalle Academy on Academy Avenue, also in Providence.

Sadly, when all was said and done, despite having some great values established and guidelines for life in place, I emerged from my Catholic school cocoon as an atheist. I do not fault the schools for this, nor do I blame it on Ozzy Osbourne and the heavy metal music I so enjoyed and enjoy to this day. My personal feeling is that as a child grows, develops, and learns, these things happen. I personally started to explore various faiths out of pure curiosity. I love sociology. I like to explore the world and learn the customs and understandings of various people across the globe. I enjoyed reading of Buddha and I marveled at some of the simple ideals in Taoism. There were things to learn in those writings—understandings that could benefit me as I grew in faith and empathy for my fellow man.

I personally felt Catholicism offered a lot of rules to be obeyed for fear of a distant boogieman who would punish you if you didn't obey. But even then, I loved, loved, loved the teachings of Jesus Christ. When one teacher I encountered dissected the parables and made them into fairytales and another spoke of the works of Christ as a heckling critic in the audience of a magician would, taking miracles and making them seem as parlor tricks, well, it was off-putting to say the least. Mix that with the way a lot of my Christian brethren would judge others and then hypercritically act—well, I had quite enough.

And so with an idea that I could carry the load of the world upon my shoulders alone, I embraced the material world and went forth. For many years, it was my way. I acted kindly, I did no harm, but I was self-focused and blind to the reality of the Kingdom of Heaven. I know I wasn't alone. Many who ventured into Catholicism have felt rejected or simply unsatisfied. Even the smallest hurdle of faith can be a stumbling block from which many do not think they can recover.

But as the bells rang in the distance somewhere past my open window, I felt a calling and an invitation to a spiritually enriched life. The emptiness inside ached to be conquered, and so the search began.

Over the next several months, I would look into various churches. I attended many but was impressed by few. All too often, I was seeing the same hypocrisy and hearing the same old rhetoric. Some seemed merely money hungry. Others forced a political agenda. Where was Christ? He was mentioned in the Gospel reading at times and occasionally in the homily, if the priest wasn't too busy speaking fire and brimstone threats from beyond, or trying out a horrible standup routine in an effort to appear fun and hip. In my opinion, church isn't meant to be entertaining, nor is it meant to give you nightmares, nor should it guilt you into donations or tell you for whom to vote. Church should teach, encourage, listen, and aide. It should inspire, nourish, and refresh. It should emphasize a relationship with God through the actions of Christ.

If you are not a Christian and are reading this, I hope you can still take something away from my viewpoints and at the very least, understand my frustration and struggle.

I finally did find a church that was what I always felt church should be. A very quaint and intimate church, in fact. The building itself was pleasant, humble, and unassuming. One did not feel the Saints nor the other parishioners were looking down their noses at them. Rather it was a feeling of community, love, and understanding.

In the coming months, seated in the last row of that little National Catholic Church, Jesus found me. I never say I found Him as He was never lost—I was. And during everything I went through, I knew God was there. The murder scene that led to the fish tank office, that led to the ambulance company, that led to the back pain, that led me there in the church. The big picture I couldn't see then and can't fully see now, but with faith, I don't have to see. He was there the whole time waiting for me to be open to Him, to step back in and fill that void. He found me and brought me back.

Time passed.

I kept up my work at a feverish pace, still without a direct goal but no longer empty. My social life continued—toned down a bit but still enjoyable.

I did a lot of crazy stuff during this time, things that made me feel alive. I took a flight lesson. I jumped out of a plane on a crisp fall day and floated above the world in a passing moment of awesomeness. I drove in a demolition derby and left my car on the track with four flats and a fire under the hood—a great analogy, by the way, for how to leave this life. I did a cattle drive in Wyoming and lived out a childhood dream perched on the saddle of a horse named Jinglebob. I always felt awkward eating steak around the campfire whilst the herd observed us with their giant tide pool eyes of black mystery. To mark the first day of 2000, I ran into the frigid January waters of Narragansett Bay with a group of men known as The Polar Bear Club. I drove solo across these great United States of America, stopping off at places of historical and personal importance.

Many of my friends had long-term girlfriends and they would soon be engaged if they weren't already. I enjoyed being a bachelor but did fancy the idea of finding my soul mate at some point. My backup plan, in case she didn't show, was to sell everything I owned and become a cowboy or live on a houseboat in the Caribbean.

One night I went to a nightclub called Prov in downtown Providence. Neither of my two compatriots wanted to venture out that night but both begrudgingly did, and in doing so, they met their wives. I bought them a round of drinks and slipped them a pen so they could make notations of the phone numbers of the women who would make them fathers.

Little did I know this meeting would be influential in my own marital status. Sometime later I was out with one of the newly formed couples to see an 80s cover band that one of their friends liked. The club was called Mardi Gras on Oaklawn Avenue in Warwick, and was composed of four smaller clubs within the one building—70s dance, hip-hop, live rock music, and a country bar. Enjoying all types of music, I started to wander throughout the clubs alone while my friends stayed in the concert venue.

As I stood in the country bar known as The Diamond Rodeo, I spotted a beautiful little brunette with big brown eyes and red pants seated next to the disc jockey booth across the floor. I bought a Corona and leaned against the bar, waiting to get her attention. A few glances and a smile later, I figured my chances were pretty good, so I took out my phone to message my friend over in the rock venue that I may not need a ride home. He didn't reply so I went back to look for him and deliver the message in person so as to not hold him up at the end of the night.

Upon returning to The Diamond Rodeo, the little brunette with the big brown eyes and the red pants was nowhere to be found. In my mind, Ralphie from the movie, *A Christmas Story*, opened his mailbox to find his Little Orphan Annie secret decoder had, once again, not yet arrived.

"Oh, stumped again!"

I combed through the other clubs looking for her but to no

avail. She was gone. Disappointed and forlorn, I ordered another Corona, stepped out onto the patio, dropped the lime into the bottle as my heart sank in my chest. As I rested my forearms on the white railings of the deck area, I surveyed the adjacent parking areas. Two lots over and heading to her car, I spotted Little Miss Red Pants and her friend. I nearly dropped my beer. I took one swig for courage, hopped over the railing, and walked ever so briskly across the sea of sleeping cars. I approached Little Miss Red Pants and her friend. They heard me and turned around.

"Thank God!" exclaimed the little brunette with the big brown eyes.

This will be easy, I thought. Boy was I wrong. She introduced herself as Desiree and I introduced myself as myself. "Allow myself to introduce... Myself." We spoke for about ten minutes about how we saw each other and why I didn't go over and talk right away. As I spoke to Desiree by name and invited her to breakfast, her friend started laughing.

Turns out her real name was Diane and she just used Desiree as her name in the club in case a guy she met proved to be undesirable. Ironically, I normally used the name Jackson for the same reason, yet that time I had used my real name. I met my match and the courtship began.

I do not divulge the details of our dating since, to me, such personal and intimate details should stay that way. I'm not the type to kiss and tell. Okay, at one time I was, but not anymore. Our relationship went through the stages many relationships do, and we kept growing closer together.

Currently Southwest flight 237 is encircling and about to land in Rhode Island, bringing me back to my sweet wife, Diane, and our family. She never looked like a Desiree to me anyway. Then again, I probably don't look like a Jackson.

As the claymation cowboy sang during Saturday morning cartoons, "After these messages... We'll be right back!"

CHAPTER 6
DONUTS

October 14, 2011

US Airways flight 1855 just finished boarding by zone. I'm in zone three and headed south toward North Carolina for this weekend's appearance. I just finished sending my customary inspirational tweet to my loyal followers of Rockstar Nation, which is the moniker I bestowed on my faithful friends, fans, and stalkers on Twitter. I always try to send out something upbeat and maybe even a simple life lesson, just in case the good Lord calls me home before the plane lands and I end up spending this Christmas in Heaven.

I think it's important to leave a legacy no matter how fleeting. Last words should be symbolic of how one lived or wanted to live. No one truly wants to go out as a cantankerous curmudgeon.

I once saw Billy Joel in concert at the Providence Civic Center and he closed his show by saying, "Don't take any shit from anybody." That always stuck with me, though I try to be more tactful than Billy Joel. It works for him though. I also send a quick text message to my wife so she knows I think of her before takeoff. Never stop dating your spouse or neglect the kids. Always be romantic and full of love.

And now, our saga continues...

So I had met the woman that would someday, two years down the road, become my wife. At this point, the yellow sticky note that I keep in my head read as follows:

2 – steady jobs
1 – mortgage payment
1 – set of solid beliefs
1 – hot girlfriend with long-term potential
What's next?
P.S. Donuts!

Donuts are always on my list, as are many desserts and snack foods. But donuts remain on the list until this day for a few reasons.

First off, they are delicious—let's not kid ourselves.

Secondly, I was once crowned the winner of a competitive eating competition having defeated several gentlemen of ample girth by eating eight and a half donuts in five minutes. I think the closest competitor ate six. I'm pretty sure I could have eaten more if I was allowed to drink milk with them, but since the competition was held at The Castle Movie Theater in Providence during a *Simpsons* animation festival, my options were limited. I took home a set of *Simpsons* DVDs for my heroic ingestion efforts. That may not have been a "dare to be great situation" but it was still pretty awesome. Throughout my life, people have underestimated me due to my slender frame. I'm not the type of guy to brag about how much I can bench, but if you ask me how many donuts I can eat, I will gladly tell you eight and a half in five minutes—without milk.

The last little tale of donuts that I will share with you goes back to my elementary school days at Monsignor Bove School. I was in first grade and still staring at the world through my innocent eyes located just beyond the bowl cut hairstyle I was once so accustomed to.

Up until that point, I had a flawless academic career. Perfect scores of 100 were written on top of my many papers that adorned the family refrigerator. As academic scholars of the first grade go, there were few more accomplished than I. If you wanted to see shoes tied with the grace of a ballroom dancer, I was your man. If you wanted to see a picture colored within the lines, hand me a box of Crayola crayons and stand back.

Alas, like many great athletes and first-rate scholars, I was cut down in my prime. A lot of lesser children would cite a growing paste addiction as the reason for their decline. I blamed advertising. My paste addiction wasn't affecting me.

Sister Florentia was my first grade teacher—an original Catholic school nun if there ever was one. She was an elderly woman with pale skin and glasses, looking frail beneath her dark habit. Every time we heard a fire engine, ambulance, or police siren from beyond the windows of our classroom, she would have us cross ourselves and say a simple quick prayer for whoever was involved with the emergency that we heard but could not see. It's something I still do today.

Anyhow, one fine day she handed me a test paper back with a 95 circled on the top of it in red ink. My heart sunk like so many pirate ships that for some reason failed to navigate around the sea monster on their map.

95? What? How? I scanned down the paper for the culprit. Surely the good sister must have made a mistake. 95? How could it be? There it was. Three quarters of the way down the page. Donut— with a big red X through it.

I didn't get it. Sister must have been slipping for sure. I was certain that on the way to school every morning, my mother drove her brown Chevy by the Mister Donut shop. It was absolutely spelled D-O-N-U-T. If Sister would just walk to the front of the school, I could point to the sign and she could see for herself.

I must have been clearly shaken since I was such a perfectionist. Sister called me up to review my paper and had me write "doughnut" next to my previous entry of "donut". When she asked me why I spelled it wrong, I called a mental audible and went with, "My pencil went out of control," rather than cite my fascination with the Mister Donut shop at the end of the block.

As of this literary misadventure, I still write it as "donut" as an homage to my first error, my youth, and my love of such delightful treats. Also, there is a Fall Harvest Donut sitting in the Dunkin Donuts bag perched precariously on the edge of my tray table right now, so it's socially acceptable.

Rest in peace, Sister Florentia. Long live Mister Donut.

CHAPTER 7
PARANORMAL INDEED

So as the sticky note said:

2 – steady jobs
1 – mortgage payment
1 – set of solid beliefs
1 – hot girlfriend with long-term potential
What's next?
P.S. Donuts!

Not a bad list for a man of 27 years. I'm sure there were many people more accomplished than I, but there were plenty doing worse as well. And I finally shirked that perfectionist attitude that dwelled beneath the bowl cut, I wasn't in competition with anyone anyhow.

Life was good but what was next? I left working in television to become a firefighter, not to work two different positions in healthcare. What was the goal now?

"And where do we go from here? Which is the way that's clear?" sang Michael Damian in the song, "Rock On". It was featured in a Corey Haim and Corey Feldman movie from 1989 called *Dream A Little Dream*. I remember this distinctly because, not only do I still enjoy the song, but it was the last 45 I ever bought. Vinyl records were on the ropes thanks to cassette tapes. Oh, how times have changed.

What was next? I had no idea but I knew I wasn't going to

become comfortable and complacent. No longer would I have to be forced from the nest. I would find my goal, take aim, and take flight. Win or lose—I was going to try. No longer a monkey clinging to a vine afraid to let go until I had my other paw wrapped firmly on the next vine—I would venture forth, take flight and soar mightily or crash to the ground, only to get back up and try again.

I was flipping through the channels one night when, quite accidentally, I stumbled across a show where a group of people investigated paranormal activity in the home of a troubled family. I was intrigued and finished watching the final fifteen minutes of the program, which then seemed to linger with me for the next few days. I had long-held an interest in spirit activity and the appearances of "ghosts", though I loathe that term.

A few of my friends and I had tried before to witness such paranormal activity at several places throughout Rhode Island over the years, trekking through the woods to abandoned ruins of houses rumored to have belonged to witches or to have been the sites of rituals and human sacrifices. Places said to be the graves of vampires or the gates to hell—those were the things that fueled my imagination and led me to read more about Rhode Island legends and folklore. I often visited many places on my own to see if I could find the truth to the stories or perhaps experience the mysteries for myself.

At this point, few if any knew that my interest stemmed from my own personal experience I had when I was about eight-years-old, give or take a year.

I was living in a house in Providence when I saw what I now would classify as a shadow figure. It stood in the doorway of my bedroom, just looming there, appearing to be watching me. Despite being in my bed, I was quite wide awake. The lights down the hallway were on, illuminating the figure from behind. The best description of it would be to picture a man about six feet tall but fill that tall frame with a dark gray mist with a shimmering effect similar to gas fumes on a hot summer day.

Being a good little Christian soldier, I ducked my head, bowl cut and all, under my bed covers and prayed for it to go away using all the prayers Sister Florentia ever taught me. I lived there another ten years without seeing it again, but my curiosity had been piqued. For what reason it happened, I didn't know.

Fast forward from 8-years-old to 27-years-old, turn the bowl cut into spiky hair that was no stranger to dye and copious amounts of product, and now you see me coming out of the ambulance company at night taking random groups of people and their friends to some of the places I had read about as s kid. I was yet to capture any real evidence and most of the time just going to get a fright and possible paranormal experience.

"Life's no fun without a good scare." Remember that from "This Is Halloween" in Tim Burton's movie, *The Nightmare Before Christmas*?

Before I had a glimpse of the show I would later know to be called *Ghost Hunters*, I had no idea there were organized groups who did what I did and were apparently even invited into people's homes to investigate paranormal activity. I consulted the yellow sticky note in my head and I made it a point to find the show again and see it from the beginning. You could imagine my surprise when I saw the Warwick water tower in the opening video montage and realized they were filming it literally ten minutes from my hometown. I quickly looked up the group and the show information online. I knew I had to be part of it somehow. I wasn't even thinking of what's next—I was just trying to get answers to my childhood experience and flying on autopilot at that point.

I emailed everyone I saw on the show but I was disheartened when days passed without any return emails. I tried again. Same result. Figuring they may be busy with production and their newfound fame, I tried emailing the team members that I saw listed who didn't appear on television. I alluded to my childhood experience, my interest in the field, my technological background, and experience with much of the recording equipment I saw them use on the show. I also attached photos of myself to show I wasn't some basement dwelling creep who survived on Diet Coke and Doritos. To my pleasant surprise, I received an email back the next day asking if I would like to meet up at a restaurant to discuss the possibility of joining the team. I was elated.

At the meeting, I went over my personal experience and understanding of the field, my limited use of the investigating equipment, and emphasized my passion for the unknown. I explained my desire to be invited into places to do investigations rather than being out tramping through abandoned places at all hours of the night.

I was granted a meeting with the team founders a short time later at a local Starbucks coffee shop on Route 2 in Warwick. I rehashed my history, experience, and quest for the understanding of various aspects of the paranormal. I was told I could join the team but would not be used on television. I assured them it wasn't a problem and I just wanted to have access to various places the likes of which I had not seen before.

A few home investigations and a short time later, I was asked to be part of the *Ghost Hunters* television series on The Syfy Channel, or as it was spelled then, Sci-Fi. D-O-N-U-T. Once again, on the television set in my mind, Mary Tyler Moore threw her hat into the air. I was going to make it after all! My imaginary Mr. Downtown shook his fist from just be on the left side of my pituitary gland.

CHAPTER 8
HERE COMES THE SUN

I just put the little yellow tag on my carry-on bag and begrudgingly left it at the top of the jetway. The flight attendant with the long brown braid is showing me and the other passengers up on US Airways flight 2208 how to use the seatbelt. She seems kind hearted and quite proficient at the art of aircraft safety.

This little plane is taking me from Charlotte, North Carolina, to Jacksonville, North Carolina, just a quick little flight with even smaller overhead storage space, hence the little yellow tag on my carry-on, which I hope is not still sitting at the top of the jetway as we are speeding down the runway. Oh well, too late now.

Here we go, back to the lecture at hand....

Out of a general interest in the paranormal, I suddenly found myself in an odd position in front of the video camera I held on my shoulder all those years at CBS and Fox news.

I did my best to be nonchalant about it, but in all honesty, it was very thrilling. I was doing something I loved, traveling across the United States for free, and I was on television. Unbelievable. I never thought of this as even an option to do with my life. So much so that I never quit my jobs. I was only on the show part time, so I simply reduced my hours when I was to go film and then come right back to work. In hindsight, this monkey didn't change after all. I was still holding on to what was safe instead of embracing what was next. They say Andy Kaufman, who was most noted for his portrayal of Latka Gravis on *Taxi*, kept his job as a busboy while he was filming the television series. Maybe we were both geniuses. Maybe we were both crazy.

I remember sitting in an SUV in the parking lot of the Holiday Inn in North Carolina while members of the cast and crew were up on the roof shooting off fireworks. I watched them streak brilliantly across the sky and then fizzle out. I worried that would be the fate of the show as well. A bright and brilliant streak across the sky that quickly faded into darkness. I didn't think that television was the proper means by which to settle down and start a family. And I was itching to put a ring upon the finger of Little Miss Red Pants.

Several investigations later, I had made my mind up. I went back to working both jobs full-time and just investigating with the team off-camera and having misadventures of my own. I even went back to work for CBS/Fox for a brief stint in order to raise enough money to buy an engagement ring. Mr. Downtown no longer worked there and only dwelled in the fish tank office in my mind. It was short-lived. I raised the money I needed, bought the ring, and bent down on one knee beneath the picturesque backdrop of the Mount Hope Bridge lit against the darkened sky, and asked Little Miss Red Pants to marry me in the rain. Thankfully, she said yes- and leapt into my arms almost before I could stand up. We were both madly in love.

A lot of people were mad too, but for different reasons. CBS/Fox was mad that I gave my two weeks' notice after my engagement. Two weeks after that, the ambulance company was mad that I wouldn't lie to the department of health about some unscrupulous practices, and so, citing financial difficulty making payroll, I was let go.

I continued on working at the surgeon's office and started doing public speaking events, lectures, and investigations with Ideal Event Management. Marc Tetlow, the owner of Ideal, had me start by doing some events for him and his company in the New England area. The money was good, the work was easy, and it kept doors open for me in the paranormal field so I could continue to investigate the unknown.

Little Miss Red Pants moved out of her apartment and into my house. Her two sons, soon to be our two sons, spent time between our house and their father's. We set a date for our wedding and started planning the big day. Time went fast.

"Life moves pretty fast. If you don't stop and look around once in a while, you might miss it." I've always liked that quote from Matthew Broderick's character in *Ferris Bueller's Day Off*. A brilliant movie.

We planned, paid bills, worked, laughed, and loved. The big day approached, and just when I thought things couldn't get better, Little Miss Red Pants approached me whilst I sat in the kitchen doing wedding related stuff and she told me I was going to be a father. Such a joy and elation enveloped my body. I would be remiss to try and put it into words. Sure there was a little issue that we weren't technically married yet, but we would be in just a matter of days, so it made for a nice little secret that only the two of us shared.

It rained the day we were married. But since it rained the night I proposed, and it rained the day I was born, I had grown to be quite fond of the rain. "Can't rain all the time," said Brandon Lee as Eric Draven in *The Crow*—a great tale of standing up for what's right with a little beyond the grave vengeance added in it.

On a sunny day nine months later, our tiny daughter was born. Fitting that the sun should shine that day as I had been placing headphones on my wife's stomach for months playing "Here Comes The Sun" by the Beatles. Our daughter is my little ray of sunshine and none shine brighter in my eyes. Lord knows I love my family, my wife, and our boys, but daddy's girl is daddy's girl and that's that.

I remember her little pink hand grabbing my finger in the delivery room, and somehow in that magical moment of wonder, she grabbed my heart.

CHAPTER 9
I'M A TRAVELING MAN

October 16, 2011

This is a test. This is only a test. I've done my preliminary scan of the passengers upon US Airways flight 2409. If somehow this flight from Jacksonville, North Carolina, to Charlotte, North Carolina, ends up somewhere in the ocean and we have to live on an island, not only would we have flown drastically off course, but I would be everyone's best chance at survival. The guy in 11F looks strong enough to be a good second-in-command—I'll have to keep that in mind. The crazy lady who insists that they deliberately asked her to take off her shoes at security just to make her day more difficult—I shall make her the Mayor of Popsicle Town located as far away from my island hut as possible.

This concludes my test of my in-flight insanity broadcast system. I'm turning up my iPod, tuning out my fellow passengers and would be island inhabitants and returning you to your regularly scheduled program.

I remember sitting in a Chinese restaurant in Smithfield, Rhode Island, the first time I heard the song "Traveling Man" by Ricky Nelson. With a belly full of wonton soup, french fries, and pork fried rice, I suddenly felt the urge to see the world. Problem being I was seven-years-old, sporting a bad bowl cut and I didn't have the ways and means to be a globetrotter. That same night, my mother, while at the Chinese restaurant, announced to my father that the bank had given them the mortgage and we would be moving out of our apartment to a new house in Providence. That house, of course, was where just a few years later I saw the shadow figure. Years later, in turn, that experience enabled me to see the world. And it started a little something like this....

"He was almost thirty. He was doing all right, though he worked all day and he worked all night. I do it all for Beans, is what he'd say. She was his tiny daughter, his sweet ba-by." These are the lyrics to a little song that I made up and sang to my daughter, affectionately known as "Beans", while I put her to sleep. The lyrics from my song were true. I was almost thirty, I was doing all right, I worked all day and I worked all night, and I did it all for her and our family.

I worked by day at the surgical office and by night I worked for the Pawtucket Red Sox as an on-field camera operator, video board operator or audio operator. In the hours between and on weekends, I had taken a position as "creative marketing director" for a marketing and advertising company. Despite my fancy title, my job was much more in depth and less glamorous. I was a salesman bringing in new clients. Together we designed a marketing plan and advertising campaign for their businesses and services. I wrote the script for the new commercials and I cast actors for those commercials as well. I bought the advertising time on the networks and scheduled the spots. I also directed the production of the commercials. Then I edited the raw footage, inserted the graphics and the music, and crafted pure awesomeness thirty to sixty seconds at a time.

I really enjoyed marketing and advertising. I've watched plenty of television, held a degree in the production of television, and I harbored an affinity for catchy ear-worm jingles and television theme songs. To be honest, I miss television theme songs. Television today relies heavily on montage footage, freeze frames, and a music bed. Long gone are the days where you could grasp the premise and underlying theme of the show just by watching its opening sequence.

Dobie Gillis was a show in the 60s about a lovesick high school student. Its theme song started with, "Dobie wants a gal who's dreamy."

"Till the one day when the lady met this fellow, and they knew it was much more than a hunch, that this group must somehow form a family, and that's the way we all became *The Brady Bunch.*" There it is—you now the backstory and the concept of the show.

"You take the good, you take the bad, you take them both and there you have the facts of life. *The Facts Of Life.*" 'Nuff said.

"Nights are long but you might awaken to a brand-new life, brand-new life, there's a brand-new life around the bend." Those lyrics closed out the opening for *Who's The Boss?* starring Tony Danza and Alyssa Milano. You could argue that it starred Judith Light, but you'd be wrong. Judith's character, Angela, wasn't the one pulling up in the blue van to a brand-new life around the bend.

There was one episode where Tony's character "Tony", a housekeeper, not to be confused with "Tony", a cab driver in *Taxi*, was picked to be in a commercial for a shampoo product. I remember seeing that episode and thinking advertising would be a fun job to have, to come up with jingles and such. But those dreams would be far from me at the time as I sat there staring at the television from beneath the bowl cut of childhood confusion.

Yet, at almost thirty-years-old, there I was working in advertising. Sadly, no one wanted jingles. "When the world never seems to be living up to your dreams," also from *The Facts of Life.*

Jingles or no jingles, I liked the work, though the hours were long and the money was not enough to quit either of my other jobs. And I was hardly awake in the few hours I spent at home. I started to wonder if I made the wrong decision by not embracing my time and possible future on the *Ghost Hunters* television program. I imagined Mr. Downtown had just left the powder room in my mind and was waiting in the wings.

At this time, the economy of the United States had taken a turn for the worst. The housing market had collapsed, people were out of work, and lots of small, local businesses were closing. Closed stores did not need to advertise. Struggling businesses could hardly afford to advertise either. Baseball season was over—no more Paw Sox. Money became a tightening noose around my neck.

"You'll never win, Pari," shouted my imaginary Mr. Downtown as he lounged comfortably upon my cerebellum, wearing sweat pants and an undershirt with pizza stains on it.

I received a call from the production company in Los Angeles. They wanted to know if I would be interested in being on a new show called *Ghost Hunters International.* Same premise as the old show but now I'd be with some different investigators and we would visit locations reported to be haunted from all over the world.

At first, the idea intrigued me. I'd get to bring to life my dream from the Chinese restaurant, see the world, and be a traveling man. I'd make some money, support my family, and take a lot of great pictures in front of some iconic structures the world over.

I looked at my daughter.

Without even giving it a night to rest or even talking with my wife, I turned it down. My daughter was only a few months old. There was no way I could do it. Forming a bond with my littlest lady was far too important and no price could be put on her.

The next few months, the struggle continued with my mornings at the surgical center, as well as afternoons, evenings, and some weekends at the production company. The news kept reporting the same old things but I could barely watch. It wasn't for me. I had no killer instinct.

I started applying for third shift jobs stocking shelves at local stores and supermarkets. No one called, and if they did, I was told I was overqualified. "Overqualified"—yeah, tell that to my bank account, my mortgage company, the credit card companies, the car loan.... The list went on and on—twice as long as Santa's—and everyone was naughty.

I was editing a commercial one day when the production company in Los Angeles called again. The first half of the *Ghost Hunters International* season was in the bag, so would I reconsider and join the show?

This time I slept on it. I talked to my wife. I prayed about it. I tried to explain and apologize to my sweet little baby Beans, who was almost one-year-old. I kissed her softly on the forehead, and with a breaking heart, I called my agent.

CHAPTER 10
GIVE US ANY CHANCE—WE'LL TAKE IT

I'd imagine that the evacuation slide on US Airways flight 1864 would be the least fun slide most people would ever have to be on, yet I would still take some joy in it, if need be. More than likely, we will land safely in the "Ocean State" of Rhode Island, but in case we don't, I'll make it a point to be jubilant upon the evacuation slide.

They're pressurizing the cabin. I best return you to your story before it becomes too intense in here. Enjoy!

"Give us any chance, we'll take it. Read us any rule, we'll break it. We're going to make our dreams come true, doing it our way!" I always liked the *Laverne and Shirley* theme song.

I may not have been doing it my way when I accepted the job as part of *Ghost Hunters International* but a few people, except Frank Sinatra, truly do. As per usual, I took the chances, broke the rules, and did what I had to do to get by- as Jerry Jeff Walker sang, "Just gettin' by on gettin' by's my stock in trade." That is the second time I have referenced that song. It is well worth your time to check it out.

We went to New Zealand to film our first episode of *Ghost Hunters International*—a very, very long way from home. It truly proved to be a test of my will, but, "If you're gonna be a bear, be a grizzly!" – The Cannonball Run 1981. Great movie.

To ease any worries in new or uncomfortable situations, I look for signs wherever I go. Little things that would only mean something to me, that would reassure me that I'm in the right place and doing the right thing. What some will chalk up to coincidence, I acknowledge as the divine.

When I arrived at my hotel in Dunedin, New Zealand, it smelled of chocolate. I checked the box spring for dead Oompa Loompa hookers but there being none, I continued my search. Sadly, I could not pinpoint the source but since the aroma was something pleasant and soothing, I wasn't too upset. I unpacked my suitcase, hung up my clothes, and placed my digital picture frame loaded with photos of my family upon the desk. I opened the window. You may not have royal trumpeters in your head that play big announcement music for your internal amusement at moments of wonder and great discovery, but I do, and I strongly suggest you have some too. As I gazed out of my window, the trumpets blasted in my mind. I imagine, Mr. Downtown went to shake his fist but quickly covered his ears as he tumbled in agony off of his cerebellum couch.

But what to my wondering eyes should appear, but the Cadbury chocolate factory! Oh happy day! What a good boy I am, thought little Dustin from under his bowl cut so many years away. Without hesitation, I made a dash for the factory just across the street. It was painted up in grand fashion with little cartoon men in little cartoon delivery trucks, delivering little cartoon bars of pure innocence and heavenly delight—Cadbury milk chocolate bars. In the window displays were smiling puppet-like cows being milk by smiling puppet-like gals. What a fantastic break from reality! I felt like a child again.

There was a tour offered that boasted a giant chocolate fountain. My mind played "Pure Imagination" as I entertained the possibility of becoming Augustus Gloop. Say what you will about Master Gloop—he got his. He knew what he wanted and when the opportunity presented itself, he pounced. Perhaps his "what's next" wasn't as complicated as ours and he could have thought it through a bit more, but he sure was happy, until the whole stuck in the pipe thing—but what a way to go. Charlie got the factory, but at what cost? Shame, guilt, and made to be the focal point of an obvious mad man's mind games. You keep the factory, Wonka, and I'll take the chocolate.

The tour was great, the samples were ample, and the chocolate fountain may not have been Wonka sized, but it did not disappoint. I made a hefty purchase of chocolate at the factory store and bought a stuffed dairy cow for my daughter. The week passed quickly and I was off to Wellington, New Zealand, to film for the next case.

I wasn't checked into the hotel at Wellington long before I found out that Poison, my favorite band from the 80s, was staying in the same hotel. Sure enough, I met everyone in the band, was given tickets to their show and a guitar pick from Mr. CC DeVille. Unbeknownst to him, he was the same guy who inspired me to come out from under the bowl cut as a child. After seeing him rock out on guitar with huge feathery hair of the bleached variety, I decided to cut my locks of childhood oppression and make my hair a signature mountain of my character. I had tried to grow it out long and feather it back but due to cowlicks and being in bowl-shape for so long, it was never to be. But with a little bit of mousse and a whole lot of hairspray, I left my bowl cut in the back of the classroom in fifth grade and embraced my signature spiky strands of awesomeness. Over the years, the lengths and colors have varied. Freshman year of high school it was probably more mullet-esque, And by junior year it blossomed to a huge shell of hair. But the attention and dedication to presentation has never faltered. One should always present themselves as best as they can.

The concert in Wellington was incredible. I was able to stand within just a couple of feet of the stage. Back at the hotel after the concert, I sat with the band, talked, and took pictures. Between the chocolate factory and the concert, all signs were pointing to my being on the right path.

Ghost Hunters International rolled on to country after country. Ratings were good. We were renewed. Within the two years of photographs that followed, you can see me standing in various foreign countries in front of various places of notoriety but increasingly behind my smile and cheap sunglasses, sadness grew and heartache helped imaginary Mr. Downtown back up onto his throne in my frontal lobe.

I traveled to many countries in Europe and South America. I visited Africa, South America, Asia, and Australia. I sent love letters to my wife and postcards to the family. I tried to video chat with my daughter so that I could at least see her and let her see me, but with the time differences, my work schedule, and internet connections that were sketchy at best, it wasn't easy.

I often went for long walks alone at night. I sat staring up at the stars with pain in my heart and tears in my eyes. Come morning, I would work out, style my hair, slap on a smile, and deliver a happy well-adjusted made-for-TV persona. Inside, though, I was dying. Despite what some people think, just because you're on television doesn't mean you're instantly wealthy, and though the money was good, with the addition of family healthcare to my overhead, times were still tough. So when I went home for the ten or so days between filming, I continued to work at the surgical office and do events for Marc at Ideal. The last thing I wanted to do when I was home was be at work and not be able to cherish every moment with my family, but I didn't have a choice. I did what I had to do. I made the most of my time with my toddler daughter. I missed her first steps. In life, there are worse things a father can do besides miss his daughter's first steps, but it killed me. It still kills me.

I felt distant from the people I knew most of my life. While I was in a different country every week, living out of suitcases and waking up in lonely hotel rooms, life at home continued and I wasn't part of it. We were finishing season two of the show and heading for season three, which would feature me in even more exotic locations, walking along in the dark, sad and alone and far from the ones I loved.

I comforted myself with prayer. I was looking for signs. They all pointed to home. Imaginary Mr. Downtown was chuckling as he drank from his goblet of misery, the run of dribble down his chin, spilling onto the floor of my mind, leaving it sticky with doubt like that of a second run movie theater.

Maybe he was right. Maybe I wouldn't win.

Being a husband and a father to me meant that I had to be there for my family, to nurture, to protect, and to guide. But it also meant that I had to provide, which sadly was a balancing act that had become so difficult that I was at my wits end.

The wheels on the bus can only go around and around for so long before they fall off… and they were wobbling.

CHAPTER 11
MALAYSIA, GHOST HUNTERS REVISITED,
30 ROCK, AND THE DREAM

October 17, 2011

"In my mind, I'm goin' to Carolina," were the lyrics Mr. James Taylor sang so sweetly. And in reality, I'm going to Carolina again. I was just there yesterday and flew home last night, but certain opportunities have presented themselves that I simply could not refuse and these opportunities require me to be in Florida tonight by way of Carolina.

So after a couple of hours in my own bed, I sweetly kissed my four-year-old daughter on the head, packed my bags, worked the morning shift at the surgical office, and now I'm safely stowed in US Airways flight 1017, for I'm going to Carolina.

As the flight slowly taxis to the runway, I'm jammed in seat 7E betwixt two passengers who are already asleep, leaving me to keep the lantern burning and watch for terrorists as I return you to the story.

Like Willie Nelson, I was on the road again. I filmed a few investigations in Malaysia, nothing particularly exciting. Truth be told, at that point, very few things excited me. I did, however, enjoy feeding the monkeys who infested a local tourist attraction. They were quite friendly and climbed up to tug on your sleeve to get your attention and your peanuts. I enjoyed my time with the dirty little primates and I was thankful for the distraction from my heartache. Some of the monkeys sat on the fence posts and simply stared at the passersby. They were probably scoping for easy prey, someone with snacks in their hands. I like to think they were gazing curiously at our opposable thumbs, hopefully not enviously as that would mean they were sad. I hope that they have emotionally evolved beyond that.

While in Malaysia, a call came in with an offer from the production company in Los Angeles to fly home early and join the domestic program, *Ghost Hunters*, for a few episodes while some cast members were out filming for another franchised program. I jumped at the chance and I was on the first flight back to the United States. No offense to the cast and crew on *International* but being stateside meant I was closer to my family, I could use my cell phone again, internet would be available to video chat with my daughter, and I could eat cuisine I understood and could digest.

So I traveled back in the U.S.A. for a few weeks. I filmed a bunch of episodes with the old crew. One of the last cases I filmed was at the American Legion Hall just outside of Philadelphia, Pennsylvania. It was a special case for me because I knew I was nearing the end of my television tenure. I had mentioned to my agent that I was running out of patience for a better situation financially and if things were going to be this tight on the road, I'd rather come home and hustle and be with my family. He offered to renegotiate my contract and see what he could get for me.

Meanwhile, the case in Philadelphia was filmed and my personal quest for answers came full-circle as shadow figures roamed the various floors of the Legion Hall just like the one I saw as a child. I didn't understand what they truly were or why they were there but it was comforting to see them and to know that I wasn't close to madness beneath my childhood bowl cut. They did exist and they still lurked about.

We wrapped filming and I returned back to Rhode Island and my loving family. My agent worked on my contract renegotiations and I worked at the surgical office as well as hustling for Marc at Ideal. All my free time was spent with my daughter and family. Like a sponge, my heart sucked up every smile, every giggle, every precious moment that was given to me.

Contract negotiations, however, were not going well. I'm not a greedy person but I could not fathom going back on the road without creating a better situation for everyone back home. I don't mind sacrifice, but to do so needlessly is ludicrous. The production company wasn't budging. They understood my position but were not forthcoming with anything beyond what my existing contract entitled me to earn. I appealed on the grounds that I simply couldn't be overseas for six weeks or more without earning more. I was heading to a dark place on the road. The only thing sustaining me was hours of focused prayer, good friends, the love of my absent family, and long nightly walks in strange towns.

So I was offered the opportunity to continue on *International* or film part-time with the domestic program. My agent continued to play the games, make the phone calls, and do his best.

I was offered a spot on the 100th episode of the domestic *Ghost Hunters* program along with a couple of my fellow members of the *International* program. We all traveled to the famed Alcatraz prison in California, filmed an investigation there, and then returned to host a live segment at 30 Rock Studios in New York City. I had always wanted to visit Alcatraz and I grew up watching *Saturday Night Live*, which was filmed at the same NBC studio at Rockefeller Center. I was very excited for the 100th episode show and even cautiously optimistic that the contract negotiations would go well so I could better provide for the ones I loved.

I traveled across the country, arrived in California, took the ferry to Alcatraz, and filmed the investigation. Despite the rich history of the place, I didn't experience any grandiose activity that I believed to be paranormal. The strangest thing that happened was almost not being allowed to be involved in the case or allowed on the island prison grounds at all. It turned out that the parks department that runs the prison for preservation and historical purposes didn't want me out there wearing my hooded sweatshirt because it was gray and white striped and they felt I was mocking the prison by imitating an actual prison uniform. I had to give a lengthy explanation that it was truly just a matter of warmth and fashion. I was glad to see they understood and allowed me to wear it on location as it would have been quite a cold night without it.

We filmed the investigation and had a grand time. When we finished up I stared at the prison walls as the ferry pulled away from the dock and returned us to the mainland, shepherding me from the last case I would film for either of the programs. I was done. This would be the end of my television career. I was, as Willie Nelson wrote, "Seeing things that I may never see again."

CHAPTER 12
IT'S UP TO YOU—NEW YORK, NEW YORK

Weeks had passed since the taping of Alcatraz. All the film was edited and things were in place at 30 Rock NBC Studios for the live 100th episode. I hopped on the train and headed to the big city.

Despite my frequent flights, I enjoy trains much more. I like the shimmy of the cars, the rhythmic *click clack* of the tracks like a comforting metallic heartbeat. I enjoy songs about hobos and I fancy traveling by train to be rather romantic and dignified. Two of my favorite albums are *Blood On The Tracks* by Bob Dylan and *On The Tracks* by Leon Redbone, who also penned a great television show theme song for *Mr. Belvedere* and a commercial jingle for All Laundry Detergent. Fantastic stuff—both his musical works and the stain lifting power of All.

I really was in awe of the studio upon my arrival. I remember staying up late with my mother and watching *Saturday Night Live* when it boasted a cast of Dan Aykroyd, Bill Murray, Chevy Chase, Gilda Radner, Steve Martin, John Belushi.... I wasn't even seven-years-old at the time but I remember lying in my pajamas, stomach down on the shag carpeted apartment living room floor, and staring wide-eyed at some of the best comedians of all time. I may not have gotten all the jokes but I laughed when Chevy Chase fell down, when John Belushi got that crazed look in his eyes, or just whenever my mother did.

And now there I was, walking around on the same stage surrounded by the same walls and sitting backstage in the green room as those heroes once did. I looked at all of the signed pictures of the various actors and bands that had performed there. I was so thankful, so caught up in the moment that the entire reality of my situation, my contract, and my pending decision didn't even register. I could never be sure but I could have sworn imaginary Mr. Downtown moved from his throne down to my eyes, standing pressed against the dark black glass of my right pupil, staring in amazement right along with me at this place of such tremendous history.

The live show came and went. My favorite part was being introduced.

"He made his usual entrance, looking so dandy and so fine." That is from *Lily, Rosemary, and the Jack of Hearts* by Bob Dylan. A brilliant song by a brilliant man.

When they said my name, I walked onto the stage, flashed a quick hello and rock star style hand signal to the crowd, stuck my chest out with professional wrestler style bravado, and continued to take my seat. I was asked later what was up with my entrance and even told that I overplayed it, but I never let anyone steal my sunshine. Let the haters hate and the jealous be jealous. It was my moment and I rocked it and I owned it like only a Paranormal Rockstar could. Plus, I knew a small child with a bowl cut watched somewhere out there in TV land.

After the show, I talked briefly with some SyFy network executives. They were all very nice and said they appreciated all I did on both shows over the years. In turn, I appreciated their kindness and faith in me through it all, continually approving my returns to their programs and pushing me to the forefront of the *International* program.

I took one last look in the green room, the makeup room, the hallways, and the empty studio with the executive of the production crew taking apart the set. I stood in the lobby with fans, signed autographs, and took pictures with them. I've always prided myself on my fan interaction, trying to reply to as many emails, Facebook posts, and tweets as I can. I always treat others as I want to be treated, making every effort to never be too busy for an autograph or a picture. I try to be inspirational in all that I say and do, not because I think I'm a big deal or that I should be a role model, but because I believe that is simply how we should all conduct ourselves; living lives of light, love, mercy, encouragement, truth, and peace.

While some people attended parties afterward and other people went out with friends, I simply returned my hotel room, lit a candle and prayed. I looked for a sign and this time it had to be a big one; unmistakable, and though I believe in the importance of understanding that God works in His time and not ours, I needed a sign that night. Tick. Tock.

CHAPTER 13
DREAM A LITTLE DREAM OF ME

US Airways flight 2257 was scheduled to bring me from gate E33 in Charlotte, North Carolina, to Tallahassee, Florida, at 6:09 pm. At 5pm, I arrived at the gate where they told me the flight was delayed for an hour. But then at 5:15 pm, I was told it's still on time to depart at 6:09 but it's been moved to gate E3. A brisk run and 29 gates later, I arrived at E3 only to be told the flight was delayed once again.

At least I ran off the fried chicken I just ate. Without further delay, unlike my flight, I return you to your story as scheduled.

Back in New York, after the live episode, I woke from a dream quite abruptly. I had my answer.

One of the most common questions I've fielded for almost two years now is "Why did you leave?" I left for a reason based on faith, a yearning for more, and because I was guided by a dream—literally. I know science wants to tell you why we dream and such but I don't buy into it. I don't see the need to explain everything. Sometimes I just want to believe. This world needs more magic, more whimsy. In a poem I wrote many moons ago, I included the line, "The death of Santa Claus is your own," and I still believe that today. Stop trying to explain everything. Be innocent. Believe.

In my dream, I was told by a friend of mine who worked in production to go talk with my executive producer. So I left the hotel in my New York dreamscape to find him and I first spotted him down in the subway tunnels. Short, salt and pepper hair, wearing a gray business suit, my executive producer carried a brown suitcase.

I tried calling to him but he didn't answer. Instead, he stepped onto a car on the subway train. I boarded the train too and made my way toward the back to find him but the train stopped and he darted out of the car headed toward another train. We lathered, rinsed, and repeated this cat and mouse cycle several times. Each time, he disregarded my shouts and walked with an increasingly feverish pace to the next train.

Finally, a train stopped and instead of getting into another car, he ran down the tunnel into the darkness. I followed him for some time until the tunnel hit a dead end. He told me all was set with the contract and he gestured to the brown suitcase.

I looked on eagerly as he opened it and revealed money stacked to the brim inside of it. While staring at the fat stacks of cash, I noticed the stark silence in my mind. The royal trumpets weren't blaring with joy. Surely they wouldn't miss an event such as this one. Imaginary Mr. Downtown should have been "boiled with his own pudding, and buried with a stake of holly through his heart," as told in *A Christmas Carol*.

Why weren't these things happening? Look at all of the money. I could finally be like Scrooge McDuck and swim through my coin vault just for fun. (Note: Two Scrooge references in one paragraph—though in truth they are worlds apart. Really sweet the way that happened.) Back in my dream I was bewildered. I raised my eyes from the open suitcase and my Scrooge McDuck fantasies only to see that my executive producer now wore a rather comical 70s style sparkling red satin devil Halloween costume. Picture a red sequin jumpsuit, complete with a hood and horns so only his mustached face grinned at me.

I awoke right at that moment. I knew what I had to do.

Internally, I recognized that I yearned to be home, to do more for my family. I wanted to do more for God. I wanted to more for others. I expected more from myself.

The devil suit in no way represented my executive producer himself as evil, but rather that my pursuit of and willingness to stay on the program for financial reasons alone was wrong. It would lead me down a muddled and darkened path with ill results.

"But you know, Bob, that will only make someone work just hard enough not to get fired," said Ron Livingston as Peter Gibbons in *Office Space*.

More money wasn't the answer. It was a stopgap measure to

problems of a material world and I had evolved beyond that. I wanted to do my own thing; something that allowed me more control, more time with my family, and more opportunity to further the Kingdom of God. Notoriety from the shows allowed me to help, inspire, and have meaningful discussions with so many people. For that, I was thankful, yet if I stayed put, I would forever find myself limited and never allowed to be in control or do things my way.

As the late great professional wrestler, Owen Hart, said, "Enough is enough. It's time for a change."

I checked out of the hotel after the sequin devil dream and hopped on the train back to Providence, confident in my guidance and my dream. Science be damned! God and guidance in dreams are real.

CHAPTER 14
PATCHING LIFE TOGETHER

October 19, 2011

My preflight iced latte is out of this world. I found a York Peppermint Patty in my laptop bag too, which means this flight just might be fantastic. The flight attendant on US Airways flight 2258 from Tallahassee, Florida, to Charlotte, North Carolina, is wearing a blue bandanna around her neck that reminds me of a great dog I once had named Belvedere. He was a little beagle pup with a love of stylish bandannas, mocha ice cream, and the ocean.

Today is looking to be pretty spectacular, as were my hopes for the future when last we left this epic tale of hope....

The good thing about never leaving my job at the surgeon's office was that I still had a position to return to after I left my two year trek across the globe whilst filming. The bad thing was my hours were extremely limited due to the fact that I spent two years trekking across the globe filming. Thanks to the notoriety of the show, on the other hand, I could work one or two public events per month for Marc at Ideal Management and still pay my bills. Of course, I knew that wouldn't always be the case, but Marc assured me that I had two years from quitting the show in which I would still be a good draw and fetch decent money to host those events.

That gave me two years to implement my plan and bring it to fruition. My plan featured two steps: begin a ministry and spread the love of Christ, and then return to television to draw exposure to both that ministry and a new, positive way of approaching assistance for those with spiritual problems.

In an effort to increase my public visibility and stay current with my finances, I also started doing college lectures as yet another side job. October seemed to be the concentration of most of my bookings and has been since the beginning because of Halloween, but the money I could make within those thirty-one days provided me a nice cushion for my family in the leaner months of the year. I thought my plan was fairly simple but executing it proved to be a completely different story.

First, out of love for God and of concern for my fellow man, I would start a ministry and travel throughout the country emphasizing a relationship with Christ and a greater understanding of the world gained through focused prayer.

Secondly, I decided I could return to television, but it had to be on my own terms. I wanted to make a show that was entertaining and honest, presented in such a way that it could be exciting to watch without being sensationalized. My increased presence on television seemed like an ideal way to build exposure for my ministry. That, in turn, would further the kingdom of God and, for at least a few, make this world a friendlier place to live.

Thanks to my agent out in Los Angeles, my contract only prohibited me from being on television for a year after my last appearance in a first-run episode of *Ghost Hunters* or *Ghost Hunters International*. This contract clause was to my advantage because I knew at the time that if the previous shows went belly up, there would be a scramble among my other costars to get solo projects going and the competition would be fierce. But, since I left before the shows ended, I had a year to get my plan together, find another production company, and get things moving for my own project.

On the spiritual front, I continued to be a lecturer at my church and I spoke with our parish priest regularly in an effort to get a deeper understanding of the readings. Luckily he always offered an easily understandable homily that was also true to the teachings without going too light, which is what a lot of members of the clergy do in order to win over less than interested people and alleviate moral responsibility. On the other hand, our parish priest never delved too much into fire and brimstone mortality that represented a vengeful God waiting to judge and condemn at every turn. The world needs a boogieman but it isn't our Savior.

I also spent countless hours listening to Christian radio, reading the Bible, and listening to podcasts by various preachers. I'm pretty sure I was the only one at the gym getting down to James Brown and then listening to gospel preachers while bench pressing. "...the one who is in me is greater than the one who is in this world." – 1 John 4:4. That not only helped me on a spiritual level but it also helped me get that extra repetition or two when I was tired at the gym.

The next step of putting together my plan to get exposure with my ministry was to open various social media pages, noting that Christ was mending our imperfections, getting us through our struggles in this material world, and catching up our relationship with God the Father and His kingdom. That continuing theme throughout my ministry work gave me the idea to call it The Patch Ministry. I decided to conduct it as a Christian ministry and not break it down further into smaller denominations, focusing on what made us the same and not focus upon our minor differences.

With the support of Marc from Ideal, we started to offer ministry lectures at the paranormal events, usually the morning after or a few hours before them. The initial support was overwhelming. It seemed a lot of people in the paranormal community had struggled with hurdles of faith for various reasons, and sadly enough, some that were strong in their faith were disenfranchised by their church for their involvement in paranormal research. I had not developed The Patch Ministry solely for those interested in the spiritual world, but if those people were in need of that guidance or affirmation, I was more than happy to help. It didn't take long for the word to spread about my offer with The Patch Ministry, and along with word spreading came controversy.

"Blessed are you when people insult you and persecute you, and falsely say all kinds of evil against you because of Me." – Matthew 5:11.

"You know they crucified Jesus too, and he said -you're not him." Bob Dylan in the song *Bob Dylan's 115th Dream*.

True indeed, that when you speak kindly about love and God you will get persecuted. Sadly the majority of my criticism came from other Christians who apparently felt the burden of living up to the judgmental reputation many have associated with the faith. I received a number of hate mail notes condemning me to hell. Some posted on websites, some on Facebook, most through anonymous e-mails that wouldn't allow for a return message, and those that did never responded to my offerings of open dialogue. For a faith founded in love, I learned what so many have unfortunately come up against over the years; there is a lot of hate. That is not to say those people and the groups they belong to speak for God. There may in fact be messengers, angels, and anointed ones, but no one speaks for God except God. But, just like in the news, the bad ones always get the notoriety and thus public opinion is formed because of them. The actions of a few allow so many people to be misled about what it means to be a follower of Christ.

Honestly, I was initially very hurt and felt that my efforts were thwarted. There were many accusations, falsehoods, and downright lies being circulated by those hatemongers in an effort to besmirch my reputation. I spoke with my Christian friends, my parish priest, other parish priests, and many long-time Christians who had also worked in researching the paranormal. Thankfully the good Lord put his people around me and shepherded me through that daunting time. I was met with words of kindness, love, wisdom, encouragement, and understanding.

One phrase has always stood out to me and I keep it close in times of trouble. "We are not close enough to the enemy if we are not close enough to draw fire." Indeed, I was under attack, so I decided my fledgling ministry must be doing some good work.

I was familiar with all the Bible verses that would be used against me due to my involvement in the paranormal. But what people fail to take into consideration, besides the fact that I was not raising the dead or trusting any spirit but the Holy one to guide me, is that one aspect of working in the paranormal field is trying to help those who are under the influence of, and in some cases, possessed by demonic forces. That is not to say I've personally had run-ins with that kind of phenomena of late, but I'm ready to do as Christ said in regards to casting out demons in His name. Funny how those against my work neglect to quote that verse.

Although the Bible is the inspired word of God, the collection of books selected to make up the Bible and some of the content within those books, was manipulated by man, and in some cases included in order to further a specific agenda by those in power at the time. As I said, I recognize the Bible as the inspired word of God, but I believe it's truly meant to stir up conversation about God, His love, His mercies, and His grace. This is a conversation that should remain ongoing to this day and beyond until His kingdom comes again.

Author Brian D. McLaren cites this very idea in his book *A New Kind of Christianity: Ten Questions That Are Transforming The Faith.* Mister McLaren is also quite controversial among what I believe to be the same circle of Christians that view me as controversial. And that's fine. Controversy can be good as long as it keeps the discussion about God going.

Holding onto the knowledge that I was doing the work I was meant to do, and with the support of those placed around me, I continued my efforts with The Patch Ministry. I used my haters as my motivators and then soldiered on.

Goal number two? Returning to television? Well, that's another story entirely.

CHAPTER 15
ANOTHER STORY ENTIRELY

It's raining against the window of row eight aboard US Airways flight 1616 from Charlotte, North Carolina, to Newark, New Jersey. It's been raining against the windows in my heart for a little bit as well. I'm missing my family as I write this, and I've been to the Charlotte airport four times in the last five days. At that point, a frequent flyer like me starts to learn the bathroom attendants by name. I drink a lot of water ... don't judge me.

Despite missing my family and becoming a temporary resident of the Charlotte airport, today has been a good one. Finding that York Peppermint Patty in my laptop bag seems to have been an omen of sorts, because now I'm sitting in an entirely empty row when I was originally booked to be crammed into a middle seat. Small victories aren't that small if you change your perspective. If you change your perspective, you just might change your life.

Speaking of change, I shall bring you back to when I was trying to set the groundwork for goal number two and change my future....

Some people in our lives are ferrymen. They are placed there to bring us from one place to another, from what's now to what's next. And for some people, we are their ferrymen doing the same favor for them. Some may not know it at the time and in truth some may never even know it at all, but the world goes around nonetheless and the good people of Popsicle Town rejoice in their ignorance. It's important to keep this ferrymen thing in mind throughout your life. Be gentle and be kind in your interactions with others. Do more than what is expected for those who can seemingly do nothing for you. You have no idea who you may inspire, no idea who you may be ferrying or who may be ferrying you; and when the ride is over, just admit that it's at its end and be thankful. Do not stand up on the shore looking back, for you will miss what is in front. What's next is not what was, but rather what will be.

My ferryman came from New Jersey. Go figure. (Truth be told, I love the Garden State even though most of Eden has been paved.)

A gentleman named Jordan Hembrough, or as I refer to him "Jersey Jordan", came into my life quite by accident. He had met a friend and fellow investigator from *Ghost Hunters International* while at a convention and he was given my contact information for possible merchandising opportunities. Jordan ran a collectible business and made a living by buying and selling nostalgia. Toys from your past, hard-to-find movie props, and an assortment of valuable collectibles were his stock in trade. Why he decided to get involved with merchandising for me is anyone's guess. My theory is he obviously has to be a gentleman of impeccable taste.

Soon Jersey Jordan and I spoke on the phone a few times and for Christmas he sent me a tin of caramelized popcorn. I wasn't too sure of him at first. As they say, don't pay the ferryman until he gets you to the other side, but he did send me popcorn to celebrate the birth of my Lord and Savior, so I decided to give him the benefit of a doubt. He made up some shirt designs for me and posted them on his website, which then led to him joining me at my events to help me sell them. Soon he became involved with others from the *Ghost Hunters International* franchise, including one Miss Angela Alderman who I worked with for a few cases overseas.

Going back to television was always something I kept in my back pocket for an idea to get more exposure for my ministry, but I definitely wasn't going to do just anything for the sake of that exposure. Jersey Jordan and I started talking about getting me on another television program. He had done some acting as a child and had recently been a consultant in some major movie productions, so he had some connections. He also introduced me to some actors like Lou Ferrigno, most famous for his role as the Incredible Hulk that I watched religiously as a child.

In time, we put together a show concept, Jordan and I, entitled *Paranormal Rockstar* that would feature me traveling through the states investigating the unknown and each week I would be joined by a new celebrity be it from film, sports, or music. Each episode would end with the celebrity guest and myself at a charity event to be held and coordinated by Marc from Ideal Management.

My ferryman from the Garden State also wrote up another idea called *Paranormal Highway*, which would feature two female investigators on a road trip checking out paranormal events. That show idea was supposed to be the vehicle for Angela Alderman and another female investigator. From Jersey, we zoom out and zoom back in to Florida where we find Angela, who also had since left the *International* franchise. She's filming a single appearance for another program as the story involved a member of her family from years past. While filming that one-time gig, she's introduced to a Mister Robin Keats and the fabric of our future is woven together. Goal number two had just had its foundation paved, unbeknownst to me all the way up in the Ocean State.

CHAPTER 16
A MEETING ON THE JERSEY SHORE

Angela won the favor of Robin Keats and put him in touch with Jersey Jordan to discuss the possibility of a future project. Jordan, then in turn, informed Robin about the show ideas he had—*Paranormal Rockstar* and *Paranormal Highway*—which resulted in the two setting up a meeting on the Jersey Shore to talk about everything in better detail. My ferryman informed me of the meeting and invited me to join them, so I hopped in Angelina, my 99 Mazda pickup truck with the flames down the sides, and she carried me to the shoreline.

While we waited at the restaurant, Jersey Jordan shared with me all the materials he had assembled for the respective programs. I played it cool and calm. Jordan, on the other hand, resembled a puppy waiting for his master to come home to let him out for a tinkle on the pink plastic flamingo in the yard. Without a preprogrammed signal like "I'm wearing a red jacket" or "I'll have a flower in my hair", we both sat in the restaurant not knowing what Mr. Keats looked like and vice versa. In hindsight, maybe I should have put a flower in Jordan's hair since he was from the Garden State after all. Every man that strayed our way and lingered for a moment was a possibility. Occasionally Jordan asked me if that guy looked like a producer, as if they all looked alike. Unless Mr. Keats brought a folding chair that said "producer" on the back and set it up in the restaurant, lit his cigarette and shouted through a megaphone like they did in the Bugs Bunny cartoons in my mind, I would have had no idea he was a producer.

Finally an older gentleman holding a folder and wearing a red jacket showed up and stood near a decorative post. Eagerly, Jersey

Jordan went over and confirmed the identity of our mystery man as the producer, Robin Keats. He reminded me a bit of Vincent Price from the old horror flicks, except this man had great bright eyes and a warm smile. I made a mental sticky note that if this worked out, I would call him "Sunshine" due to my perception of those attributes. I like to give people nicknames. I cannot remember real names but names I give to people in my mind seem to stick there.

So Jordan and I sat across from Sunshine at a restaurant table and explained the concepts. No promises were made but we signed limited option agreements so that Sunshine had our permission to shop the shows around for further development and production.

Three months later, that option agreements were running out and it looked like my forecast was more rain, not Sunshine.

CHAPTER 17
SUNSET ON A DREAM

US Airways flight 1685 is one of those tiny little prop planes where there are single seats on one side of the aisle and two seats on the other. I enjoy these planes the most because the flying seems more authentic, more of a real experience in contrast with the jumbo jets on which I usually fly. I've always had a kinship with the underdogs in any situation and that apparently extends to planes. I support Donald Duck over Mickey Mouse and Daffy Duck over Bugs Bunny, for example. "Perhaps being number two means that you try harder." Linus Van Pelt wrote that in his letter to The Great Pumpkin as shown in my favorite autumn special, *It's The Great Pumpkin Charlie Brown.*

I've been home for less than twelve hours in seven days, my eyes are burning and "I'm so tired I haven't slept a wink. I'm so tired, my mind is on the blink," as John Lennon sang in the Beatles. There are nine people on this flight, which makes my mind shift to another song on the record player. "Number nine, number nine..." Also a Beatles song, which you will find a lot of in my brain. And if this flight was blown off course and I ended up stranded on an island, I would once again have the best chance at survival. "They are the egg men. I am the walrus. Goo-goo-gachoob." My mind shifts to another Beatles song as I have gauged my fellow passengers on this flight.

All right kids, begin dream sequence—we are going back to a time when a new show was not to be and goal number two may suffer a heart wrenching blow as we waited on Sunshine so we could go walking on sunshine and it would be time to feel good....

As I said, the pitch contract we signed was for three months. Sunshine told us that if we couldn't get someone to sign on to it by then, it was ours to bring elsewhere. Sunrise, sunset, quickly go the months. Three months slipped past us without a deal in place. By the time our initial deal was up, Sunshine asked in good faith to just give him a bit more time without any new paperwork to sign, without anything official, but just a gentleman's agreement. I have always been a man of my word and Jersey Jordan had not given me any reason to doubt him. I just had a gut feeling that Sunshine was a man of his word as well, so we had an agreement.

In the meantime I still had bills to pay and so the hustle continued. An event or two a month for Marc at Ideal Management, the surgical office by day, and Pawsox games on nights and weekends filled my calendar. Autumn came and baseball season ended just as college lecture season began. The guys at GP Entertainment had a solid schedule for me that entailed traveling as far south as Florida and as far west as Wisconsin with a dozen stops in between. The lecture money was good and I liked talking to the crowds. I always mentioned my work with The Patch Ministry and it pleased me to speak with so many students about the Christian faith after my lectures were complete.

The only downside to doing the lectures was the extensive travel. The two weeks leading up to Halloween were a muddled kaleidoscope of planes, rental cars, college campuses, and lonely hotel rooms. Flight delays often had me sleeping on airport floors. Tight turnarounds had me sleeping in the rental car in truck stop parking lots as the chilly night air frosted my windows and my soul. But I knew I had a warm bed at home and a house full of people that loved me and depended on me, so I curled up with my jacket as a blanket and did what I had to do, as I have always done.

Autumn gave way to winter, and with it I acquiesced to a reality in which my what's next was not a return to television. I applied for numerous positions in various fields. Retail stores and warehouses again told me I was overqualified. Most places didn't call back at all. Unfortunately my media connections within Rhode Island didn't have much to offer me either. The bills were piling up as the holiday noose tightened. Feeling trapped under financial burdens, I called Jersey Jordan and told him I was out and the deal was off. He tried to talk me out of it but I stood my ground. He agreed to keep working with Sunshine and see if something developed. I wanted nothing more than to do my work on a larger scale but I also knew my limits and the limits of my family. I couldn't wait around for years for a dream that might never come true. It wasn't fair to them.

I called upon my father to use his connections to find me a city job that paid a decent wage and offered a pension plan so that I had something to look forward to for retirement. I figured I could do whatever job came along and continue my ministry efforts on the side. If things became tight again, I could always hustle through another part-time job.

I went and met a state worker at a diner. He was a longtime acquaintance of my father's and could offer me a position driving a dump truck for the city. After my father quit driving tractor trailers, he had settled into a longtime position driving a dump truck and it had provided very well for our family over the years. All I had to do was pass my commercial driver's license test and I would be good to go. I kind of fancied the idea of taking my lunch to work with me every day and then sliding down the back of the dinosaur when the whistle blew at 5 PM—just like Fred Flintstone.

Weeks passed. I studied the handbook for the CDL test and I made peace with that path in life for me because it gave me a means to provide for my family. It may not have looked glamorous but it was honest and steady work. I've never defined myself by a job title. And anyway, a job was just a job. It served its purpose.

I had one more lecture scheduled in the off-season down in the New York/New Jersey area and so I put off my CDL test until after the return from what I envisioned as my swansong on the college lecture circuit.

But just then, Jersey Jordan called. He had heard from Sunshine and met with his partners, Sunshine's wife, and a gentleman named Ron Ziskin. They apparently believed in the *Paranormal Highway* show and wanted to insert me into the driver's seat with Angela Aldermen riding shotgun. Of course I was a bit torn as I had all but given up on the show. I had already purchased myself a plaid thermos to take soup in for my dump truck adventures, yet Jordan talked me into meeting with him and the people who wanted to produce the show after my last lecture.

I said my prayers, drank my milk, and took my vitamins like Hulk Hogan told me to do through the glass of my television screen many years before. I packed my bags and headed to my lecture behind the wheel of my black workhorse, Angelina, who was pushing 200,000 miles at that point.

What awaited me down the highway was a mystery.

CHAPTER 18
YABBA-DABBA-DOO

November 4, 2011

Delta flight 4175 is bouncing through the friendly skies as I make my way from Providence, Rhode Island, to Washington DC to do a gig in Virginia. I just came home two nights ago from a weeklong trek of lectures.

Let me waste no time with clever verbiage and tongue-in-cheek puns, but rather expedite you back to a meeting of the minds after what I thought was my last lecture.

"Not bad for a La Quinta," was a line Stewie Griffin uttered in an episode of the animated show *Family Guy*, and those were my thoughts as I made my way to the hotel lobby for my meeting with Ron, Sunshine, and Jersey Jordan. I stopped to fill a few Styrofoam plates to their breaking point with the hotel's continental breakfast. Meetings are meetings; they will always be as such, but hotel continental breakfasts usually end at 10 AM, so if you want a stale cheese Danish and a make your own waffle, sometimes meetings have to wait. With three plates in my hand, I sat across from Sunshine with Jersey Jordan on my left and Ron on my right. Since I had stopped to make my own waffle, there was only one seat left which left me with no decisions and put my back to the door. It must be the cowboy in me but I don't like my back to any door at all. However, Ron had a certain quality that was reminiscent of Lorne Michaels, the longtime executive producer of *Saturday Night Live*, and with that in mind, I trusted he would watch the door without speaking a word.

I received praise from the group about my lecture the night before. They said it was insightful, but more importantly, it was funny, which was an aspect of my lecture that they didn't expect. I remember eating my mediocre waffle and wishing my wife was there to hear it. After a few years of marriage and seeing me day in and day out, she formed a decidedly stubborn opinion that I'm not funny. Such a wife I have.

Ron outlined the plan to take a clip reel of Angela and I, and then shop it around to a few networks, including Syfy where my previous television appearances have been. Contracts were produced and placed in front of me. They said I needed to sign posthaste.

At that moment, my phone rang and I took my half eaten waffle and excused myself. Since it was my mother calling, I had to answer it no matter who had that meeting with me that day. The waffle was god-awful, so I trashed it. On the other end of the line, my mother cried because my aunt had taken seriously ill and she wasn't given much time. I did my best to comfort and calm my mother but there wasn't much for me to do from the lobby of a La Quinta besides make another subpar waffle.

With a heavy heart, I hung up the phone. I've always been one to handle death pretty well, or as well as can be expected. I don't see any shame in crying and grieving, but for some reason, be it a matter of faith or what have you, when someone of an old age begins the process of leaving the material world, I become very thoughtful and prepare myself to accept the course of things. Fortunately I have never lost a family member in a sudden tragic way. I think that would unnerve me quite a bit more and I pray I never find that out. My aunt was known for having a heart of gold. Full of whimsy, love, and optimism, she was always the life of the party and a bright beacon of hope in dark times. She was also my godmother and one of the first people I ever encountered who shared my fascination with the paranormal and the love of the Halloween season. She also believed in me and delighted in telling everyone that I was her godchild and on television.

So I sat down at the table again and said not a word of the troubling news until after I signed the paperwork and handed the pen back to Ron. I knew my aunt wouldn't want me to give up. It looked like Mr. Slate would have to find someone else to work at the Bedrock Quarry.

CHAPTER 19
AN INTERNAL LIGHT OF HOPE CANNOT BE EXTINGUISHED

In the few months that followed, my aunt drifted in and out of hospitals. I visited her and brought her food from the outside. It struck me in the most intense way that whenever I visited her just how positive and upbeat she remained throughout our conversations. I told her of upcoming network meetings and she introduced me to every nurse, doctor, and orderly that came into the room because she was so proud of everything I had accomplished. We talked about family and life, struggles, and triumphs. I may not have been there to visit her as often as I should have, but the time we did spend talking was of great substance and guidance, which remains an inspiration for me today.

One night, with my wife lying in bed beside me and my darling daughter, Beans, snuggled in between us, the phone rang. I took my cell phone into the other room and closed the door as to not stir the little one. It was Sunshine. Ron and the team had inked a development deal with the Syfy Channel.

"Things are going to start happening to me now!" That was Steve Martin in *The Jerk* when he joyously saw his name in the phone book for the first time.

I contained my excitement in order to not wake up the house. I hung up the phone and went back to the bedroom and kissed my wife, relayed the good news and kissed my daughter on the top of her head. Things were going to start happening to me now!

I started a "what's next" campaign on my various social media websites before the ink on the development deal was even dry. Early promotion is a key element to buzz marketing. I knew that the contract did not necessarily guarantee me a show but I believed in it and so would everybody else.

On the next visit to see my aunt, she was not very responsive. She held her eyes open briefly and only said a few words. I slid my right hand into hers as she lay there in the bed. I told her how much I loved her, how much she meant to me, and I told her she was the best godmother I could have asked for. She was my "Gourdmother"- a nickname I had given her due to our mutual love of Halloween and the traditional gourd decorations. Then I told her about the contract and the new show idea.

She squeezed my hand, opened her eyes, and smiled. I said what I knew would be my final goodbyes and set out to make her as proud of me as she had always been from the first day of my life.

CHAPTER 20
CRAMPED FLIGHTS AND TWO-DAY PILOTS

November 5, 2011

As US Airways flight 3396 prepares the cabin for takeoff, I'm preparing myself for home sweet home. I just finished my last lecture and public event for the year of 2011. I will be home working my job at the surgeon's office throughout the remainder of the year. I'm looking forward to time with my family, uninterrupted by travel. Speaking of uninterrupted—back to our story.

With the network signing the developmental agreement, the next step was shooting the pilot. My agent had negotiated me a fair deal and was even able to get me a position as a producer on the new show, *Paranormal Highway*. This meant a lot to me as it was important that I show people I was more than just a pretty face, as they say. I wanted to put my own stamp on the show. I wanted to have more say in what the show was about and how it was presented. Since I had a degree in television production and exposure, I knew I could really do the job and not just receive a vanity title like so many others.

Sunshine had an idea for the first case. We would travel to New Mexico and investigate skinwalkers, a very powerful and terrorizing force according to Navajo legend. Skinwalkers were said to be medicine men gone rogue. They switched to the dark side and would emulate the forms of various animals as they frightened and sometimes murdered the Navajo people. Being out on the West Coast, Sunshine had the contacts to make it happen. Being on the East Coast, I did research on the legend of the skinwalkers. I made phone calls to various tribe members I knew and trusted. Sunshine set up interviews, tracked down leads, investigated stories, and secured the location for filming.

A date was set for August 15, 2011. We flew out to New Mexico and shot for two days and two nights straight. I was exhausted. Being a cameraman for so many years, it wasn't until I stepped in front of the lens that I realized how much work being talent, or should I say "good" talent really was. Keeping your energy level up and trying to cover your emotions in situations, not only verbally but also with your body movements and reactions, becomes very tiring. It's especially tiring when you're on tight reality show budgets, have been sitting in a cramped airplane for several hours between mountainous people in miniature seats, survived two layovers, and have had four hours of sleep. The emotional and physical drain on the body and spirit is very real.

However, I am chock-full of awesomeness. I never give up. I'll never surrender. If there's a job to do, I'll get it done no matter what the odds may be.

So in two days, we filmed what could have been an entire episode from start to finish. To put that in perspective, it usually took two weeks to make one episode for *Ghost Hunters* or *Ghost Hunters International*, and even that was pushing it. Shooting a full episode in just two days was nothing short of amazing, though exhausting.

I'm not one for complaining, unless I'm overtired or I haven't been fed—I'm a little bit of a child that way. I remain thankful for the God-given blessings and opportunities that have come my way.

I returned home and checked in regularly with Sunshine and production. They loved the footage and I received praise for both my on camera talents and shooting ability as I did some of the filming. All that was left to do was wait for the edit to come together and then hear the network's response.

Tick. Tock.

CHAPTER 21
TURN AND FACE THE STRANGE CHANGES

Maybe I'm easily pleased. Perhaps I'm more optimistic than most. I'm determined to find a smile living on every gray cloud caught up in the jetstream over my head. I've only walked out of three movies in my lifetime: *Blank Man, Speed Two: Cruise Control,* and *The Eternal Sunshine of the Spotless Mind.* I'm very tolerant.

So when I received the copy of the first cut of the *Paranormal Highway* pilot, I was overjoyed. Outside of a few edits I thought could have been tightened up, I was thrilled with it. Keep in mind, I often turned in my rough drafts of my writing throughout school and for the most part I despise movie remakes. Whilst in marketing, I also hated when I worked on a project for three weeks and then after the final edits, some miniscule critique by my client's 8 year old son like "I don't like the color blue in that graphic," forced me to change it all up. Hence why I left marketing. So when I was told we had to await a second edit before the network brass could view it, I tried to be patient. I appreciated that production thought highly enough of it to strive for excellence. After all, it's not like we would be getting another chance.

A few weeks later, Labor Day weekend came along and I attended a wedding rehearsal. A friend of my wife was getting married and my sweet little bride was to be the matron of honor in that ceremony. My phone rang with that ever exciting 818 area code, which meant something was happening since no one, except Sunshine, ever called to just chit chat. On the other end of the line was production asking if I could do a conference call in a few minutes to discuss the networks feeling of the reel, so I took down the information for the call and stepped outside.

With all the major players on the line, I was told that the network loved it and that I was specifically to be told that the president of the network said I was "frigging awesome" (he used a harsher expletive but I like to keep things PG-13 at best). There was an air of excitement as well as a rumor of a series order of twelve episodes, and lots of good feelings being exchanged. It was honestly the only conference call I've ever enjoyed. Usually conference calls are a cluttered mess of people talking over one another and no one waiting to yield the floor to the next speaker. Everyone is a tough guy from the cold and darkened safety of their own basement.

I usually just sit quietly on the line and listen. Sometimes I close my eyes and pretend I'm a pirate and the roaring voices on the line are just waves crashing across the bow of my mighty vessel. I speak up if there is something I feel strongly about, of course. I'm like a horse that way. Mr. Ed would also never speak unless he had something to say.

But this call was different. We laughed, we congratulated, we waited for what's next. Sunshine and I were asked to write up twelve episode ideas to bring to the network.

I could hardly wait to get started! This thing was about to happen.

CHAPTER 22
THESE THINGS DO HAPPEN

Weeks had passed since Sunshine and I had submitted our episode ideas, to the deafening silence of no news. I called, I e-mailed, and I waited. Nothing. I knew something was amiss, yet no one talked to me. I grew frustrated.

Around October of 2011 I headed out to do my college lectures as I usually did, which was good as it was a chance to catch up on bills and store away some money for Christmas, but it was also tough as it meant I was about to spend a week and a half on the road mostly in a rental car. I was thankful to the guys at GP Entertainment for lining up so many speaking engagements for me but to keep things as profitable as possible for my family, I had opted to drive everywhere in the rental car rather than spend money on flights. I usually drove for eight to twelve hours a day in order to reach my next college campus. I slept in a hotel for an hour or two, washed up, arrived on campus to deliver my lecture, signed some autographs, took some pictures, and then climbed back into the rental and headed back out on the road, or back to the hotel if I had time. Many times I simply didn't have enough hours to stay at the hotel, so I just slept in the rental car parked somewhere on the roadside. My wife and family worried, so I learned to just tell them I was at a hotel and not curled up under my jacket in the driver's seat.

I come from a long line of hard-working men who have done what they had to do in order to provide for their families, and despite the little bit of notoriety I had received, I was no different.

Finally, the 818 area code appeared on my phone as I drove through the twisted roads of the West Virginian mountainside. The variety of bright autumn colors that lined the road would make you think you were navigating through God's box of crayons, which was a vivid contrast to the harsh black-and-white news I received on the phone that day.

Somehow, after a test audience had seen the demo reel, I had gone from "frigging awesome" to "boring" and "unattractive". I had an "objectionable hairstyle" and they also didn't like my taste in clothes, particularly my "mom jeans" and "printed t-shirts". I imagined Mr. Downtown jumped with joy upon the saddened floor of my mind. The news nearly made me drive off the road since I had been so congratulated and led to believe everything was fine. The news for Angela, my original cohost on the show was even worse. They were going to move forward with the show but they wanted to discuss replacing the cast.

"Mom jeans?" I wore my usual rock star style ripped up jeans similar to what I had worn for many seasons on *Ghost Hunters* and *Ghost Hunters International.*

"Printed t-shirts" sounded too eerily reminiscent of the real Mr. Downtown criticizing my rock and roll t-shirts back in my news days. For the demo reel, I had worn a black t-shirt with a raised black design of a family crest and a white t-shirt with a black ink blot design. Why do people hate t-shirts so much?

At any rate, I was told to sit tight and see what would happen. I finished my college lectures up and returned home slightly crestfallen, heartbroken, and confused. A week had passed and they made it official, calling my cohost and telling her it was over. I hung onto my hopes and I remained positive. If it wasn't going to work out, then there had to be a reason for it.

"These things do happen," as said in the *Phantom of the Opera.*

I had settled back in at home and had picked up more hours at the surgeon's office. I did a few events for charity. The air turned cold and the trees lost their leaves. Thanksgiving came. Turkeys died. I felt saddened as I drove by their empty pen at the turkey farm on my way to work and I blew my truck's horn in memory of the fallen feathered comrades whose only crime was being an icon and being delicious.

My old truck needed tires badly. All of them were bald and one was being held together by copious amounts of Fix-A-Flat, hope, and dreams. I had to put air in the tire every three days or it would go flat.

One of those cold mornings as I was huddled over the air compressor in my driveway and looking at my reflection in the quarter panel, my phone rang—818.

CHAPTER 23
VISITED BY THREE SPIRITS

I was told after things had settled down that they realized there wasn't anyone with more credibility, knowledge of the field, skill on camera, talent with a camera, and production capabilities than myself. Their words, not mine. Whatever. Apparently I was "frigging awesome" again. Maybe the client's son who didn't like the blue graphics had to admit he didn't really know what he liked. Maybe the cosmos aligned in such a way that it became apparent one test audience reaction could be errant when considered in comparison with the previous ones of which there were numerous.

I was told the female investigator had to be recast but they wanted to keep me on the project if I would allow for concessions regarding my hair and wardrobe. It's important to note that, although previous shows may portray me in a "pretty boy" light, I in fact do things more for comedic value than for personal concern. However, I do not like to make changes as they pertain to doing things for the mere approval of someone else. I said I could dress up my wardrobe a bit in the way I had in the past with an overthrown dress shirt, creating a layered look. I conceded that I could trim my hair down a bit too. In truth, I only said this because I had just gotten it cut and knew they would want to see some photographic evidence.

You must think I'm kidding.

You'd be wrong.

I put away my air compressor and headed back into the house. A quick visit to my closet and what do you know? One uploaded photograph and it's confirmed that I'm "frigging awesome" again.

"How very silly," I thought.

I tried my best to get my original costar back but I had no leverage, and sadly there truly wasn't anything I could do but hope her path had a bright future and that God would take care of her as was His plan.

They wanted to try and schedule a shoot with a new woman, and perhaps add a third person to the mix. We would shoot in early January of 2012 so the network to get a feel for the cast interaction. Details would be discussed later as they pertained to location and such, so I had time to enjoy Christmas with my family. I hung up the phone and thought about being on the road at Christmas time. I recall being in an airport in Singapore on Christmas Eve and hoping beyond hope that there would be no delays so that I might have Christmas with my family; that I might be there to hold my daughter in my arms and see the smile on my wife's face.

The future is unknown to all of us. I don't care what your local Susie psychic says. Who knows where I maybe next Christmas? But the present I had a hold of- and I was going to have a great Christmas at home with my family and no regrets.

CHAPTER 24
AND HERE WE ARE

January 6th, 2012

I am aboard US Airways from Philadelphia to Los Angeles. For the first time since I started writing this book back on October 2 of 2011, I am up to date and so are you. I can no longer cleverly foreshadow or bury a witty little "there, I know what will develop" in the chapters ahead. I have no idea as to what's next. Sorry I didn't write on my first flight from Providence to Philadelphia but I had my James Brown music up loud and I was dancing. As the blue skies envelop this aircraft and puffy white clouds hover just outside of the windows, I sit here in seat 10C—the exit row. Lots of leg room and lots of wonder as to what is ahead of me.

I am hopeful, as always. The fact that I spent $36 on the upgrade to exit row seating is a testament to the fact that I believe this will work out, as I normally am very conscious of how much gets spent and where it's spent. I also want to be on top of my game for tomorrow's shoot.

This is it.

Two years of work has culminated in this moment.

The line in the sand has been drawn.

There's a lot at stake here. More than just a little television show. It's about the fundamental well-being of my family, first and foremost, as well as the ability to spread the word of my ministry and to inspire people to live better lives. My opportunities on television or in production going forward from this project will be directly affected by the success of it. Increased notoriety for myself will lead to more work for people who have supported me and believed in me over the years. Most importantly I'd like to be able to tell more people about my ministry efforts and help lead more people to a positive life surrounded by the love of God.

There is a lot at stake for sure.

Worried? Nah. And that's not just playing it cool. That's straight talk right there.

I believe in myself. I am confident. I know I'm doing things for the right reasons and that I'm operating and acting in truth and love. Plus I know that whatever is meant to happen will happen when it's supposed to happen because that's how things happen. Can I say happen enough?

People can talk. People can mock. But it's more than a belief. It's an honest understanding. It's a realization of truth. Things happen as they should in the big picture. If tomorrow goes horrible, I still have jobs to go home to. I can still hustle. I still have a family that will love and support me for years to come. Things will be great.

Tomorrow I'll be working with Miss Jael De Pardo, who I have worked with before on her previous program *Destination Truth*. If the network likes us together, we go into series. If not, we go home. She and I have since gotten back in contact and are mutually excited as to the opportunity that is before us. She has taken an interest in how all this came to be and she is supportive of my vision of what is and what can happen with this project. Though I do feel sadness for the loss of my former partner, I couldn't be happier with the network's decision to add Jael to this new show.

So here goes nothing.

Here goes everything—again.

And here we are.

CHAPTER 25
YOU MUST BE THIS TALL TO RIDE

January 8th, 2012

As I sit on board this US Airways flight 959 from Los Angeles to Charlotte, North Carolina, I am very, very tired.

Yesterday—filming day—started at 9 AM when I left the hotel and ended around 2 AM as I returned to the hotel. What occurred during the shoot was nothing short of insanity. Fasten your seatbelts by inserting the metal piece into the buckle, pull the strap down tight, and hold on kids because we are experiencing turbulence.

The production assistant had been up in front of the hotel to pick me up promptly at 9 AM as scheduled. At 9:02 AM, my cell phone rang. It was the production company informing me that Jael wasn't able to make the shoot. We had two options in proceeding without her. They said I could get back on the plane, fly home to the East Coast, reschedule the shoot, or I could work with someone else who was also under a contract option agreement with the network.

The other person? Jack Osbourne. As in Ozzy Osbourne's son.

It wasn't a tough decision, really. Jack had name recognition and he had previous experience on television. He was the son of the legendary rock star, whose music had shepherded me through the trials and tribulations of high school. Plus, I really wasn't ready to hop back on a giant metal bird and fly back home. I trusted that this was another instance of divine intervention and a twist of fate once again in my roller coaster of life. You must be this tall to ride.

With everything official, Jack was going to meet us in a drugstore parking lot on our way back to the shoot location. As I rode back to the location, my mind became a cluttered toy chest of questions. Is this the way it was supposed to go? Would Jack and I have the right chemistry on camera? Would we be compatible off camera? Did Jack have any real interest in the paranormal? I don't want to come off as a snob but the paranormal field means a lot to me and I don't know if it means anything to Jack. When would I get to meet Ozzy and Sharon?

I knew the shoot we were doing was a complete mockup. It was never meant to be a true investigation—just a fabricated case to show the network how we looked on camera together. But the interaction was important. If we were going to sell this show, we needed to come across as true friends, or at least two people who had met more than five minutes before in a drugstore parking lot. I wanted it to feel real.

Up pulled a beautiful white Porsche and out stepped Jack Osbourne in khaki pants and a blue and white plaid shirt. I laughed on the inside because he wore the exact wardrobe the network had asked me to wear. Good thing I didn't listen and wore my ripped jeans and t-shirt anyway. If I had worn what they asked me to, Jack and I would have looked like fraternal twins whose mother dressed them alike.

Jack and I were introduced and then took part in a brief production meeting. While we set up our gear and loaded tapes into the cameras, we had a few crucial minutes to speak. After brief pleasantries, I had to bite the bullet and simply ask him about his interest in the paranormal world and the show. I wasn't trying to be disrespectful or rude but the thought was in my mind that Jack came from a very well-known family of substantial fame and wealth. I'm the son of a truck driver and a housewife who are also well regarded but in much smaller circles.

So was this just something to do for Jack or was he really into the field and the concept behind the show? Because I had two years into this and not a dime to show for it, so I took it seriously. I was relieved to hear that not only did Jack like the show concept, but that he had a true interest in the field, knowledge of many legends and entities, and that he had also spent the night in many locations I was aware of or had investigated myself.

What unfolded in the hours that we filmed consisted of on-camera banter and off-camera conversations that will hopefully be part of the next chapter of *Paranormal Highway*, of what's next.

Jack showed a great sense of presence whilst in front of the camera and grace off of it. He laughed politely when I joked that, if the show didn't make it, I'd make a great personal assistant. And he didn't raise an eyebrow when I started singing an Ozzy song that came on the radio before I realized what I had done.

As we were filming, my thoughts were peaceful, most of my questions answered, and so it was that I would wait to see how things developed. We sat together at one point and Jack pointed out some graffiti on a rock that read, "I want things to feel real." I didn't let on to him the importance of that sign and what it meant to me. I simply snapped a picture of it and knew another question was answered. This was the way it was supposed to go.

We had finished filming everything together by 8 PM. Jack had to take his leave and I stayed behind to film with two other guys from a casting company in case the network decided to make it a three-person show. The rest of the night was dark, cold, and without too much excitement, except my ankle getting twisted, which still throbbed as I came back to the hotel at 2 AM.

CHAPTER 26
HANG LOOSE

February 24, 2012

Southwest flight 496 from Providence, Rhode Island, to Denver, Colorado, features me in row 21, seat D, although this row is empty, so at any time I can raise the armrest and become 21E or 21F. Perhaps I could become a different person entirely and alter my reality. Anything can happen. At any moment we are all capable of change. The smallest of actions can lead to the biggest of alterations and vice versa. Our environment changes. Our reality changes. Our understanding changes. The only constant is the evolution of the unknown, whether we want it to or not. That's important to keep in mind. Our survival depends on it. Our mental wellness hinges upon it. At the click of the secondhand as it swoops across the face of the clock, the sands of time blow across our mindscape and our reality forever altered. For better or for worse, you have to adapt. You have to feel, to understand, to live, to reach beyond your grasp, letting go of what's now, and stretching out into the darkness to achieve what's next. Never giving up. Never surrendering. But evolving, adapting, surviving, understanding, and achieving. Each decision matters. Every moment counts. Don't waste a second.

Tick, tock.

Tick, tock.

I'm currently flying to Colorado to do an event at the Stanley Hotel. It's an enchanting place in its own right with gorgeous mountain views, bright sunny skies that make you want to breathe deep, and a McDonald's in the lower plaza parking lot that offers a fantastic pancake breakfast. They are notoriously stingy on the butter, however, with a little prodding, more is available.

Somewhere between pancakes, mountains, and seat 21D, my mind is wandering. My understanding of reality, of what is and what is not meant to be, has been a Rocky Mountain landslide of confusion since last week.

It was February 13 and I watched television with my wife, as our daughter lay sleeping on my arm. "Carry On Wayward Son" came pouring into my right ear from my cellphone atop the nightstand. It was Sunshine. I excused myself from our bedchamber and went to take the call.

Robin, who I call Sunshine, informed me that he had heard from an executive at another production company that the network was hot for our show and crazy about Jack Osbourne and me. We should be expecting a call to make things official very soon. I thanked Sunshine and went back to share the good news with my wife. Imaginary Mr. Downtown begrudgingly turned out the light behind my pituitary gland and prepared to make his exit. I had just snuggled myself back under the covers when Kansas decided to play an encore on my cell phone. I saw the 818 area code of the production company and quickly excused myself from our bedchamber once again. I joked with Little Miss Red Pants upon leaving that I knew they said it would be made official soon, but I never thought this soon!

Ron, my other executive producer and partner in crime was on the line. As the production company was patching in the network executive, Ron said two words to me in a quick hushed tone: "Hang loose."

I imagined Mr. Downtown lingering at the threshold of the shadows of my mind, suitcase in hand.

CHAPTER 27
THE MAN BEHIND THE CURTAIN AT CORPORATE

"The show is over. Close the storybook. There will be no encore. And all the random hands that I have shook, they are reaching for the door." Those are the opening lyrics to a song called "Colorful" by The Verve Pipe. This played in my mind while I waited on the line.

The network told me how much they loved me. (I knew something was wrong at that point.) I was told how much everyone appreciated my work on this project and previous shows I had done. (I was being dumped.) I was told what an outstanding professional and incredible person I was. (It's not you.... It's me.)

In the end, the network was going forward with the show, my concept, my ideas, and my episode pitches, but I was no longer going to be on it. Imaginary Mr. Downtown flipped on the lights and slammed the door on his way back in, shattering my mental window of peace and my dreams in one triumphant swoop, dashing back to the throne in my cerebellum, knocking over some half empty cans of Diet Coke that seeped through the sticky floorboards in my brain and pooled up behind my eyes. The network asked me to stay on as a producer for the project as I was still a valued member of the team and my insight would be helpful.

"Hang loose," indeed.

I was stunned. Two years of work. Two years of believing and sacrificing and hustling.... For what?

My mind raced trying to put words together. Incredible decisions of incalculable importance were being made at fractions of a second. One hand was clenched tight, fingers folded in rage. A younger version of myself would have burst forth with a verbal tirade that would have made the most foul mouthed comedian blush. My other hand remain slightly open, both to hold the phone and also in passive acceptance.

It wasn't all bad. Originally, I was only pitched to be the on-camera talent but I fought and negotiated for weeks to be a producer. I would still be involved in something I worked so hard to bring to fruition. I would still be compensated and be able to provide for my family. Plus, as a producer only, I wouldn't have to travel as much, which would in turn give me more time to be with the ones I loved, and also, leave the door open for more opportunities: my "what's next".

I thanked everyone for their honesty and for the kind words. Of course I would stay on as producer. I did have to ask one question, however. If everyone I was involved with loved me so much, why replace me as talent? Not that I have a huge opinion of myself in a grandiose sense but what was the reason for taking me off camera since I had the notoriety and solid reputation in the paranormal field? They told me everyone at the network was on board for me to be talent but a guy up at the corporate level did not see it that way and he stood at the top of the ladder. So the guy behind the guy behind the curtain got to make the call- whether anyone actually knew he existed or not. Such is this life. It's a good thing I live for more than this world has to offer.

We said our farewells and said we would be in touch once my spot was recast. I hung up the phone. I looked at my reflection in the mirror. I put my hands over my face and whispered "your will be done God" in a quick prayer and I shuffled off to bed, thankful that my wife was asleep. I knew she would be supportive but I wasn't ready to talk.

As I walked around to my side of the bed and pulled back the covers, imaginary Mr. Downtown did his best to bellow a hearty, "You'll never win, Pari!" through the painfully abandoned hallways of my mind, but he nearly choked thanks to the celebratory cheesy puffs he had hastily stuffed down his slimy gullet. I flipped him the imaginary bird, which I knew wasn't the appropriate or Christian thing to do, but I didn't feel too bad about it as it was imaginary and no one is perfect, after all.

I kissed my daughter as she lay sleeping. I texted Sunshine and Marc from Ideal Management, both of which had long ago started as business partners but had shown their true colors as kindred spirits and close friends. Both were shocked and confused, especially Sunshine, who had, only an hour before, thought we were good to go with the show as we had planned it.

The disappointing news churned around in my mind as I turned on the television and put on a *Twilight Zone* rerun that I had saved on my DVR. It was called "The Odyssey of Flight 33" about a plane that jumped back in time and flew over a seemingly foreign landscape complete with dinosaurs. It wasn't my favorite episode of *The Twilight Zone* but it somehow eased my mind and seemed to fit.

In many ways, my understanding of time had just disappeared. I found myself back two years ago with Jersey Jordan and Sunshine working on a show and wondering what's next.

Before I closed my eyes that night to say my prayers and thank God for the blessings in my life, even those I didn't understand, I picked up my phone one last time and sent a text to Sunshine. I told him about a new show concept, new format, new ideas, and would he be interested? He replied, "We'll start first thing tomorrow."

CHAPTER 28
THIS IS NOT THE END

As I sit here in seat 21F—yes, I've slid over to the window seat—I sometimes find life and words and words about life are easier to ponder whilst observing puffy clouds with edges that appear almost indefinable. I'm thumbing carelessly yet thoughtfully through the preceding pages of this Captain America composition notebook that I wrote this literary misadventure in. Anything could have been written betwixt its covers. Whoever purchased it could have used it for their purposes whether that be grocery lists, a diary, or even a book of their own. I certainly didn't know what I was going to use it for when I bought it. I just thought it looked cool.

I've always liked the idea of Captain America, yet I can't say I've ever read more than two or three of his comic books. I did like the movie though. I'm all about doing what's right over doing what's easy or what's only right for me. Risking it all at the drop of a hat to defend what is the upstanding solution to any roadblock is how I choose to live. I think that's what Captain America means to me, and so on that notion, I've purchased many Captain America t-shirts over the years and this little notebook, which ended up chronicling one of those times in my life filled with whimsy, ferrymen, uncertain seas, distant shores, and dreams.

In each of our lives, there are many voyages such as the one you are reading—people not as fancily documented with insight and insanity but they occur nonetheless. When I began writing this book, I had no idea what would be written or how it would end. Just as a new blank page greeted me, a new day greets us all. We can write whatever we want. We can aim for whatever goal is important to us at any given time. Find your "what's next" and work toward it every day. Be passionate. Be fiery. Exhaust yourself in pursuit of it. Through setbacks, through pain, through cheap shots taken at your expense, hold your head high. Start fresh every day. The new page. Another chance. The most important lesson to impart on anyone is the ability to learn from our mistakes but in no way be prisoner to our yesterdays. Always move forward and never use a crutch or lean on excuses. Always evolving. Always stretching, reaching, and growing. Never, ever stagnant.

We are all capable of achieving truly great things. Most often what holds us back from what's next is ourselves. Either we are too afraid to try, we are too complacent to move forward, or a variety of other man-made roadblocks of nonsense and negativity. We don't pursue what's next. We are simply programmed to accept what we can touch in the here and the what's now.

I say never settle. Always strive. Accept what uncertainty or sense of duty you may have to accept, but try to use it in relentless steps forward toward your goals. Enjoy what you have and be thankful for it but always push yourself for more in matters that are truly significant. Do not get caught up and weighed down with glittering anchors of this material world.

Be wise enough to know that people are meant to be loved and things are meant to be used, not the other way around.

So where am I going from here? Well, when the plane lands I'll do the gig at the Stanley Hotel. I'll shake hands, pose for pictures, and sign autographs. I'll stand tall on the stage and answer the usual questions. I'll share a little bit about myself and what I believe in and I'll make the usual jokes. Then I'll take groups of people along to a mini investigation of the hotel as they look for paranormal activity. Through it all, I will be hoping a few of them, or at least one of them, will find something more. Through their interaction with me, I hope they'll take away an understanding of what it truly means to live life to the fullest each day, always in positive pursuit of what's next.

How am I doing? As Kenny Loggins, the godfather of movie soundtracks, sang: "I'm all right. Don't nobody worry 'bout me."

Of course I was more than a bit disappointed with the way things turned out. For two years I had envisioned myself as the talent and producer of *Paranormal Highway* but as it turned out, I couldn't be both of those things. I fought all I could for it for as long as there was opportunity. I'm smart enough to know when I'm being steered in a new direction. Achieving the level of producer was important to me and I did that. Seeing the show through from an idea until it was reality was what I wanted to do, and it looks like that will happen (as of writing this page, at least). I wasn't going to bang my head against the wall and force the on-screen talent issue, nor was I going to throw a pleasant little pity party for myself and use it as a crutch, as an excuse for why I never did anything else.

The man behind the curtain at corporate doesn't define who I am. Only God does. I get to play a small part, stylistically speaking of course.

Do you know who Dick Rowe was? Historically, he is noted as the guy who passed on giving The Beatles a record deal. He was the guy behind the curtain at corporate and, as you may know, the band went on to do quite well. The names of John, Paul, George and Ringo are well known by billions of people. And so, I'll continue to sail the dark and stormy seas of the unknown for now because beyond there are tranquil waters. And, after all, I am the walrus. Goo-goo-gachoob.

I'm continuing on doing the things I want to do and the things that are most important to me. Just as I knew I would when I was back in the high school guidance counselor's office. Just as I knew I would when I was a mere boy under a bowl cut staring at the television and animating my reality.

I'm a husband. I'm a father. I strive to inspire others. I'm a fairly good Christian soldier and I continue my work in ministry. I'm thankful for everything I've been blessed with- and if the big guy upstairs invites me home tomorrow, I would have no regrets. But as long as I'm here and there is breath in my lungs, you can bet dollars to donuts—D-O-N-U-T-S—that I'll relentlessly pursue what's next, what's right, and I will be carrying the torch of awesomeness in the fight against misery, never giving up, and never surrendering.

EPILOGUE

June 2, 2014

The thing I enjoyed most about the documentary film course that I took whilst enrolled ever so briefly at Rhode Island College in 1995, besides the beauty of Judy Garland in *Meet Me in St. Louis*, was the way most documentary films take you in one direction, end up going in another, yet they somehow reinforce their initial objective and teach a wonderful life lesson. Come to think of it, why did we watch *Meet Me in St. Louis*? That's not a documentary. Maybe the professor had a thing for show tunes. I'm not sure.

Anyhow, here I am, seat 20D on the aisle and just behind the wing. Willie Nelson, that red-headed, beautiful gypsy bastard is singing "It's A Bloody Mary Morning" through my Jack Skellington ear buds as Delta flight 1211 tears a path through the afternoon sky, taking me to Detroit on my way to, ironically enough, St. Louis, Missouri. Huzzah for serendipitous writing!

What's in Missouri you ask? Let me… "show you".

Get it?

Missouri is known as the "Show Me" State. Better living through puns—that's my motto. Well, one of my mottos anyway. The other ones don't apply here, but they are equally awesome—though some of them are a tad on the naughty side. Hey, I try to be good, but an angel I surely am not. If I have a halo, it's a bit askew and balancing on tiny horns.

I am on my way to film the first of a short series of *Ghost Hunters* episodes, now in this their tenth season. More on the reason for this flight in a moment. Let's get caught up, shall we? Surely!

(Don't call me Shirley).

A lot has changed between when I began this book and now. The handsome notebook emblazoned with Captain America that held this literary misadventure betwixt her thin cardboard covers was nestled away in my bedside night table drawer for over two years just awaiting the right time to be edited by the right person. Special thanks to my dear friend turned editor, Miss Jessica Jewett, for tackling this beast (despite her sending me pictures of my prized notebook laying on her bed with a bottle of girly nail polish balanced upon it!).

I always knew it was important to put this book out there, perhaps more so for me than for anyone else as its autobiographical portions are important documentation for my daughter, Beans, to read someday when she is older, and maybe again when Daddy hath long been eating pumpkin pie with Jesus and Elvis in the cloud palace just North of New Jersey. Funny thing... Christ doesn't like whipped cream upon his pie, but He will take some right from the can. Can't argue with the guy—for several reasons.

So I sent out the handsome Captain America notebook to young Jessica in early May of 2014, with instruction to edit it to the best of her ability whilst not losing my "voice" in the piece. The rough version of this opus is filled with scribbles, arrows and asterisks. God bless her for deciphering it at all. But since she is a trusted friend and someone I speak to on the regular, I knew the messy thoughts that is my inner author's voice would be preserved like that mosquito trapped in the amber in Jurassic Park. Her extraction of the mosquito's DNA has produced this T-Rex. Roar, baby, roar!

Whilst this book was being edited, I was contacted in the end of May 2014 by the people at the production company of the ghost show and I was asked to return to the ever shrinking small screen. Though it was very nice to be asked, and actually kind of humbling to still be seen as relevant television talent after not being on camera in about five years or so, my initial thought was to not do it.

Since last I had written anything for this book, life has worked out pretty damn well. I licked my wounds after the ole' Hollywood screw job had taken place. *Paranormal Highway*, which was to be my show, turned into *Haunted Highway* with Jack Osbourne, who most unfortunately was diagnosed with multiple sclerosis a short time into filming the first season. Though Jack and I never had opportunity to speak again after that initial filming, I never held anything against him, and I wish he and his family all the best. God bless you Jack.

The show went on to air for two seasons with various on camera talent. I sat at home, collected a producer's fee and enjoyed being with my family—weary, but wiser. They took the show in a completely different direction than my vision for it and never used any of my ideas. Their loss.

I continued to work part-time for the Pawsox baseball team until this season. I had put in over ten years working for them in one capacity or another. My daughter asked me to stop working there at the end of last season so I could spend more time home with her at night. I considered it over the winter and tendered my resignation before the start of the 2014 season. Though I have many fond memories of the ole ball park, it was the right decision. I ended the 2013 season with them in grand fashion. They held a Halloween Night at McCoy Stadium in September, not quite the right time, but it felt like Halloween nonetheless. People came in costumes. Vendors handed out candy and I was asked to throw out the first pitch, something I had always wanted to do whilst watching the game from behind my video camera or from up in the control booth for the past ten years. Yet, when it came time to go out to the mound, my wife and little six-year-old Beans by my side, I couldn't do it. I bent down, gave Beans the ball and let the little girl who held my heart have the baseball and make the throw. She came up a tad short of reaching the plate, as you'd imagine a six-year-old would, but she never missed in reaching my heart. It was a magical moment for me, and hopefully for her as well.

As fate would have it, due to an unexpected occurrence on my way to McCoy Stadium last year for job number two, more magic happened. I ended up appearing in a Dunkin Donuts commercial, resulting in enough of a financial windfall that I wouldn't miss the extra income normally provided by my position at the Pawsox. Funny how God works that way.

In late April of 2013, I stopped at the Dunkin Donuts on Division Street in Pawtucket to grab myself an iced latte betwixt job number one at the surgeon's office, and job number two at Pawtucket Red Sox. I always would opt for a little go-go juice to get me through these 15-17 hour work days. On this particular day, I accidentally locked my keys in my truck whilst fetching my beverage. I returned to see my keys on the driver's seat, leaving me with no way into my truck. I placed a call in to my wife and asked her to bring me the back-up set. It should be noted that this is not an unfamiliar happening in my life. My wife and the good people at AAA have often been summoned for this exact occasion. Believe it or not, I am rather scatterbrained.

Since I had some time to kill, and it was a bright sunshiny day, I climbed into the bed of my truck, and took to Twitter to update my fans and friends on my latest happy misadventure.

"Accidentally locked my keys inside my truck while stopping at Dunkin Donuts. So now I'm sitting in the back of my truck, sipping my latte and smiling." Little did I know that this particular tweet would be read by someone at the ad agency for Dunkin Donuts, resulting in me being contacted in September of that same year, and then doing the commercial. I'll spare you the details of the commercial shoot at McCoy and up in Boston, with this one exception: they let me use my own truck! Sweet Angelina and I were in the spot together. I was so proud of my ole gal. That 1999 B3000 Mazda and I have ridden the road to hell and back together on our journey to 300,000 miles and this was a great detour along the way.

In other news, it turned out that keeping my position as an anesthesia technician while filming all these shows, doing these lectures, and event appearances, paid off after all. The doctors at MSL Surgery asked me to be their Practice Manager, and COO of the company, also in September of 2013. September has always been graciously kind to me, whereas April has always robbed me like a thief. Such is my life. This position in the corner office (actually one of only two offices) is one that I had been working toward and was very happy to finally achieve.

I now manage two offices between Rhode Island and Massachusetts, and the practice is doing well, with signs of growth yet to come. It's very enjoyable for me as I can choose to sit in my office listening to my James Brown music if I want to, or I can go out onto the surgical floor and still assist in surgery if the mood strikes me. I enjoy variety and appreciate having options in all aspects of life. It keeps it interesting.

With all of this in place, it was not a black-and-white decision in regards to coming back to film *Ghost Hunters*. I was very content at home. I like my daily routine of hitting the gym in the morning, working from 8-4 or even 5 or 6 in the evening, and then coming home to tackle my little daughter and smother her in kisses. We have a nice dinner together as a family. My daughter and I sneak downstairs for some video games while Mama Bear gets the tub ready for the little one's bath. I get them off to sleep and then I have some me time. There are night time walks along the woods with a crisp pumpkin ale, or happy little jaunts through the cemetery with hard apple cider disguised in an unassuming plaid thermos. I catch up on my reading, my writing, and NASCAR. I hustle some paranormal events or motivational lectures at least one or two weekends a month. I get to help others.

Life is good.

So, leave this and go back on television? Nah, thanks but no thanks. I would like to thank the academy for the nomination, but I can't see leaving all of this. So, with those thoughts dancing with the sugar plums in my head, *Ghost Hunters* discussions and negotiations went on for the better part of two weeks. I have to hand it to the production company—they are persistent if nothing else. After praying about it and discussing it with my family and employer, I decided I would do a short run of episodes just to help out the ole team and have a little fun. A short run of appearances of my choosing would allow me the freedom to maintain my daily routines for the most part and not affect my career. I have four weeks of vacation time at my disposal with my new position, so I may as well put it to good use. While most people would utilize that to sun their buns on a beach somewhere, I will go and walk around in the dark and have a good time. In the process, I will make a little extra money to do the things that need to be done around the house, contribute to the nest egg to replace my dear sweet Angelina after she reaches 300,000 miles, and most importantly as it pertains to finances and their use, I will stash away enough money to take my family to Disney World again in 2015. Riding through the Haunted Mansion with Mama Bear and Beans by my side is one of my favorite things. It's right up there with brown paper packages and whiskers on kittens.

Don't get me wrong, regarding my hesitation to return to the ghost show, I really do enjoy being in contact with the spirit world but I can do that any day, anywhere, so the investigation portion is just a bonus. The unseen spiritual realm is around us at all times. It is alive, more so than we are now. It is boundless and glorious. It is everything and then some. I'll see you there someday. Look me up. We can grab a slice of pie at the malt shoppe with Frank Sinatra.

What I am really hopeful will come of this selective return to the bronze screen is that perhaps, perchance, it will grant me the ability to cast a wider net, grow my social media influence in an effort to further expand my motivational speaking and faith-based lecturing opportunities. I like helping people. It's just what I do. I have a helpful heart. And I'm thinking this limited edition run of mine will allow me to help even more people in this struggle of life.

I truly feel that it is the charge placed upon every soul as it travels through this human experience to aide, to walk with, to fall with, and to grow with, the others that are here at the same time. In all aspects of who I am and what I do, I exist in kindness and in love, with an honest aspiration to change the world, if even only for a few people.

It is my honest and sincere hope that this book, this little slice of happy nonsense, has somehow done that for you—that this book has somehow brought you joy, hope and understanding. If nothing else, maybe there was at least one thing that made you smile, for in this world, there exist too many people to whom you could give the Mona Lisa and they would complain about a scratch upon the frame. Don't be like them. Find things to be happy about. It's really not that hard. Dance in the rain because it's the elixir of life. Smile in defiance because you should never let the bastards get you down. Don't let anyone steal your sunshine. Never allow anyone to hold the key to your heart in their back pocket. This is your life. These are your dreams and if you don't make them a reality, no one else will. Most importantly, enjoy the journey.

This world is full of waitresses waiting to be actresses and only then will they be happy. I say, be happy whilst you are a waitress. Enjoy each small moment. Laugh over every dropped plate. Grin and bear every tip you receive that is less than 15%, for no one is promising you tomorrow and there is much to do today. Each twist and turn of fate that you come across, is a chance to learn, to grow, and to live in love. Have a goal set for yourself in the future but don't live in that future until you get there.

Now is your time. Take the stage and give the performance of your life because it is your life whether you can see the crowd or not. Whether they are booing you or cheering you matters not, for one way or another, you are getting a reaction- and if you are being true to yourself and to the greater truths of this life as they have been shown to all of us in the quiet corners of our dreams, then you are doing just fine.

I hope that some of the stories from my past that were presented in this book have helped shed a little light on the happy nonsense that is my life, and perhaps explain why I do the things I do, and why I believe to be truth that which I now know to be truth. Somewhere within the pages and lines of this literary misadventure have to be a few gems in the rough which can be mined, polished, and put to good use if for nothing more than decorative paperweights in your own cluttered mind.

Wave your freak flags high, my friends. Each one of your perceived imperfections are the fingerprints of your creator and He made you different for a reason. Keep your eyes on that horizon, and when you ship doesn't come in, swim out to it. Don't float there treading water with self-righteous indignation, for the world has enough people like that already. Encourage those people to swim, but if they must sink, let them do so on their own. Don't let them wrap their darkness around you and pull you down into the murky abyss of misery with them.

As for the culmination of this book, I think it is a bit like a documentary film. I started out with hopes for it to be going in one direction—a happy tale of redemption, proof that the underdog can overcome great odds and come out a winner, and a true story that would end with our hero returning triumphantly to television with his own show, saving his family from the cold, hard rocks of financial ruin, all whilst standing for what he believed in. I wanted to compose something that would inspire people to never give up, but rather to stretch in faith, to reach out into the unknown darkness of the future to grasp the elusive swinging vine of "what's next" in their own life. I wanted an ending where I would see myself in my mind's eye standing with a foot upon the dead, bloated carcass of Mr. Downtown, somewhere behind the couch of my mind's cerebellum, just next to the gray matter, back and to the left.

But alas, as most documentaries film go, if I remember them correctly and I hadn't actually enrolled in a film study course solely focused upon the theatrical efforts of Judy Garland, this story did in fact take a turn I did not expect, and now it would appear that it still has resulted in the relaying of the intended message and then some. You see, all has worked out, perhaps in a rather different manner than the live studio audience in my mind had anticipated, but it worked out nonetheless.

Our hero did do the things he really needed to do. Funny enough, though I see it now as severely unimportant, I am going to be back on television on my own terms and available for a limited time only, just like Boo Berry cereal, my favorite breakfast treat.

Thanks to me being at home and not on the road the last few years, I was able to aspire to a great position at my place of employment, thus securing the finances necessary to provide for my family for years to come. Though I personally believe that shiny rocks and bits of paper with dead people upon them are empty idols useful only in their manmade purpose of trading for goods and shelter, money is, as they say, a necessary evil. I may not be Rockefeller but through the grace of God, I manage to pay the bills and get us through to the next month, and the next, and the next.

And if I squint just a little, like a pirate looking out over the misty waves of his salty mistress as she blinds him with the reflected beauty of the sun, I can see myself in my mind's eye standing with a foot upon the dead, bloated carcass of Mr. Downtown, somewhere behind the couch of my mind's cerebellum, just next to the gray matter, back and to the left.

D. Pari... victorious in the battle against misery.

For you my friends, you must understand this: we live these seemingly chaotic lives of randomness, yet they bury us in neat little rows. Our lives are littered with what we dismiss as coincidence and happenstance, as we are unaware that these are the things that bend us and shape us the most in this human experience.

We cannot see the big picture from our human viewpoint. We cannot see that truly nothing is without a plan and that somewhere out there, off beyond the swirling popcorn stars and the rotating rocky rings of Saturn, God is snuggled warmly beneath His blanket of humanity, resting comfortably in what He has woven, in what He has designed. "For all the world is a stage and we are merely players," and so on and so forth according to wee Willie Shakespeare.

That's all I have for you my friends. Thanks for reading. I wish you all the love and kindness in this world and the next.

Dream big. Work hard. And most importantly, never give up. I love you, you beautiful, beautiful bastards.

And so, I offer you this simple phrase for kids from one to ninety-two, though it's been said, many times, many ways… smile, damn it! It's only life after all. - D. Pari

ABOUT THE AUTHOR

Dustin Pari was born and raised in New England, where he makes his home with his wife and daughter still today. In addition to his career in health care he enjoys his work as a motivational speaker, Christian lecturer, and paranormal researcher. Dustin has co-authored two books about the paranormal prior to this work. He prides himself upon being an industrious spirit with a kind heart, and a smile for all he meets.